REMARKABILIA

Concerto Macaroni

REMARKABILIA

Compiled & annotated by

JOHN TRAIN

Illustrations by Pierre Le-Tan

Foreword by Bernard Levin

London
GEORGE ALLEN & UNWIN
Boston   Sydney

George Allen & Unwin (Publishers) Ltd,
40 Museum Street, London WC1A 1LU, UK

George Allen & Unwin (Publishers) Ltd,
Park Lane, Hemel Hempstead, Herts HP2 4TE, UK

George Allen & Unwin Australia Pty Ltd,
8 Napier Street, North Sydney, NSW 2060, Australia

First published by George Allen & Unwin in 1984
Published by arrangement with Clarkson N. Potter, Inc.

Remarkabilia is based on John Train's
Remarkable Names of Real People or How to Name Your Baby, 1977;
True Remarkable Occurrences, 1978;
Even More Remarkable Names, 1979;
Remarkable Words With Astonishing Origins, 1980.

British Library Cataloguing in Publication Data

Train, John
  Remarkabilia.
1. Curiosities and wonders.
2. Names, Personal
I. Title
001.9'3   AG243
ISBN 0–04–808050–0

Set in 11 on 13 point Garamond by Nene Phototypesetters, Northampton
and printed in Great Britain
by Butler & Tanner Ltd, Frome and London

FOREWORD

(Reproduced by kind permission of *The Times*)

We are always told that it is rude to make jokes or other adverse comments about people's faces or names, as no one can help either. Since neither half of the proposition is true (anyone can change his name, and the variety of aids to face-amendment is constantly growing), I have never seen the force of the rule, though on the whole I have obeyed it, if only for the sake of peace and quiet. So when, a few years ago, I stumbled across a little American book called *Remarkable Names of Real People*, by John Train, I said nothing, though the book consisted entirely of a list of names which excited mirth without any additional comment at all.

Now, however, doubtless encouraged by the success of his first volume, Mr Train has published a sequel, *Even More Remarkable Names*, and I can no longer refrain. The whole thing started with a letter from a lady in Florida who wrote to a local academic to enquire whether she had the funniest name in the world: her desire for reassurance on the point was understandable, in view of the fact that she was called Mrs Verbal Funderburk, but the book was destined to give reassurance of a very different kind – by the time the reader has finished it, the good Mrs F. might as well be called Smith or Jones for all the impact she makes. Indeed, so amazingly rich is Mr Train's collection that he can afford to throw away in the introduction to his first volume such figures as Mac Aroni, Cigar Stubbs and Virgin Lands, and to relegate to the humble status of footnotes in his second such figures as Legitimate Jones, Vernal Equinox Grossnickel,

Zeditha Cabbagestalk, Halibut Justa Fish and the siblings Bump and Twinkle Quick.

But what would you? The first volume starts with A. A. A. D'Artagnan Umslopagaas Dynamite Macaulay, and goes on almost immediately with Ave Maria Klinkenberg and Bambina Broccoli. The editor then rather spoils things by including Bathsheba Finkelstein; I will have him know that my celebrated Bessarabian grandmother was called Bathsheba Nemkovsky, and anyway Bathsheba is one of the most beautiful of names, whatever it may be followed by. But Miss Finkelstein is followed in volume one by – I now begin to quote at random, there really being no other place to quote at – the Reverend Canaan Banana, now President of Zimbabwe (though President Ould Daddah of Chad is unaccountably omitted), Daphne Reader's Digest Taione (who reminds me that there is a town in Arizona called Truth and Consequences, after a television quiz-game of that name, though I suppose the inclusion of place-names would have extended the volume too far, possibly even as far as that town in New Zealand, from which I occasionally get a postcard, which is awesomely entitled Levin), Charles Adolphe Faux-Pas Bidet, Gaston J. Feeblebunny, Halloween Buggage, Madonna Ghostly, Mark Clark Van Ark, Trailing Arbutus Vines and Zoda Viola Klontz Gazola.

But that was only the first shot. *Even More Remarkable Names* includes Aurora Borealis Belsky, Cardiac Arrest da Silva, Christ T. Seraphim, Easter Buggage (daughter of the Halloween Buggage in the first book, and born between the two), Ecstacy Goon, Eucalyptus Yoho, Hector Spector, Heidi Yum-Yum Gluck, Hogjaw Twaddle, Pirouette Spiegel, Odious Champagne, Solomon Gemorah and John Hodge

Opera House Centennial Gargling Oil Samuel J. Tilden Ten Brook. Oh, and Pepsi Cola Atom-Bomb Washington.

Now it must be stressed that Mr Train insists on documentary proof of the existence of these people before he will include them in his compilations; difficult though it may be to believe, therefore, there really are (or were, for he includes dead but verified examples, too) people who go or have gone through life with handles such as these. It is vain to speculate on what precisely, or in some cases even approximately, their parents thought they were doing; it is equally vain to feel that they ought not to be made mock of; *our* guilt will not help to cure *their* neuroses. But of course the only point in writing a column on a subject like this is to go one, or better still several, better.

We who dote upon Beachcomber's *List of Huntingdonshire Cabmen* and the Seven Red-Bearded Dwarfs (who included Sophus Barkaya-Tong, Edeledel Edel, Frums Gillygottle and – oh, I might as well give them all – Scorpion de Rooftrouser, Churm Rincewind, Cleveland Zackhouse and Molonay Tubilderborst) are hardly likely to be impressed by Plato Foufas, Mrs Tackaberry McAdoo and Thusnelda Neusbickle, from Mr Train's first volume, or Loch Ness Hontas, Lavender Hankey or Earless Romero, from his second, genuine articles though they be, and a nation which has in its time had Mr Denis Healey as its Chancellor of the Exchequer will not consider Mr Train's work done until a third volume includes that memorable Siamese finance minister of some years back, Prince Dam Rong.

Ian Mackay, the great *News Chronicle* columnist, once dug out of some ancient newspaper files the result of a competition to find the most remarkable real name, and he printed a selection of the finalists, though without much hope, as he said, of convincing his readers that he hadn't made them up. Which is not surprising in view of the fact that they included Septimus Bug, Fish Fish and Through Trial And Tribulation We Come At Last To Heaven Slappe.

My family used to know a New York family which, in the first flush of enthusiasm for freedom's newest ally in the 1940s, named their son Joseph Stalin Pomerantz; only the other day my eye fell upon the striking moniker Brigadier O'Brien Twohig; for years and years I used to think that the famous Irish solicitors, Argue and Phibbs, were apocryphal, until somebody sent me a letter he had received from them; and Herbert Kretzmer of the *Daily Mail* insists that there is a man in the Nairobi telephone-book called Theanderblast Mischgedagel Sump, though it is only right to add that I do not believe him.

It is the same Kretzmer, incidentally, who told me the lamentable tale of George C. Ziglbauer, of whom I was reminded when I came across Gisella Werberserch-Piffel, a Hollywood actress, in Mr Train's compilation. George C. Ziglbauer was a well-known Hollywood figure in the thirties, I think in some lesser but essential trade such as make-up or set-building, who was constantly suffering teasing, jeers and ridicule because of his name. Eventually, he could bear no more, and changed his name to Sinclair, which did him little good, as he was ever thereafter known throughout the industry as Upton Ziglbauer.

Once, staying with Quentin Crewe, I plucked down *Who's Who* and read aloud, in sonorous tones

(I subsequently set the whole thing to music), my favourite entry, which reads, in part:

Sir Jamsetjee Jejeebhoy, 7th Bt; son of Rustamjee J. C. Jamsetjee Jejeebhoy and Soonabai Rustomjee Byramjee Jejeebhoy. Succeeded cousin, Sir Jamsetjee Jejeebhoy, 6th Bt, and assumed name of Jamsetjee Jejeebhoy in lieu of Maneckjee Rustomjee Jamsetjee Jejeebhoy. Chairman, Sir Jamsetjee Jejeebhoy Charity Funds, Sir Jamsetjee Jejeebhoy Parsee Benevolent Institution; Trustee, Sir Jamsetjee Jejeebhoy School of Arts, Byramjee Jejeebhoy Parsee Benevolent Institution. Heir: Rustom Jejeebhoy.

Blow me if Quentin didn't promptly cap it by bidding me turn to:

Sir Olateru Oba Alaiyeluwa Olagbegi II, the Olowo of Owo, son of Oba Alaiyeluwa Olagbegi I; married, many sons and daughters; Educated, Owo Government School; Treasury Clerk in Owo Native Administration; Address, PO Box 1, Afin Oba Olowo, Owo; Telephone number: Owo 1.

Bernard Levin

PREFACE

Art can never hope to surpass reality. I hope this collection of remarkable names, extraordinary words and curious episodes will show that the real world is much more bizarre than the inventions of the richest imagination.

According to the Egyptians, the god Ptah made the world by naming every person, place and thing. As he uttered each word, creation sprang into existence. Certainly Ptah should be the tutelary deity of name-fanciers (or onomasts, as they are called). A parent, naming a child, partakes of this power.

As most people know instinctively, there is indeed a curious magic in names. Call your little one *Elmer*, and he will be less likely to succeed than if you plunge in with a *Charlemagne* or a *Napoleon*. (Had the Emperor been christened *Gaston* he would surely have remained stuck as an obscure officer of artillery.)

General *Ulysses* Grant . . . what panache! Led by a *Hiram* (the General was in fact christened *Hiram*) the boys in blue would have cracked; President *Oscar* Lincoln could not have held the Union together. There would have been no Bicentennial. And speaking of panache, one knows that if Rostand had not celebrated *Cyrano de Bergerac* but *Paul Blanc* he would have flopped in the provinces and never made it to Paris, let alone to immortality.

The singular confections now chosen by many American families for their infants are not as remote as one might think from the customs of an earlier day. Before the Conquest the inhabitants of an English village would devise a novel first name for each child that came along, like yachts or racehorses, so no family names were needed. Thus, only a handful of English kings before William the Conqueror – or Bishops of London, as one sees from their tablet in St Paul's – bore the same name as any of their predecessors. After 1066, however, England's new Norman masters required that all given names be drawn from a hagiology of about two hundred recognised saints. Then as now, the choices were not distributed evenly over the whole spectrum, but clustered around a few particularly popular ones, e.g., William. This meant that in all but the smallest hamlets, duplications occurred, so surnames became necessary.

America is heading the other way, towards the elimination of surnames, particularly in the younger generation. Today's kids, one gathers, were devised by parthenogenesis, or perhaps in the lab, without paternal intervention. 'Dad this is Jennifer and Nicole.' Parent, *sotto voce*: 'Jennifer and Nicole *who*?' Child: 'Huh?'

As the family sinks into *anomie*, and family names with it, a broader repertoire of given names will be required for identification. The present volume will, we hope, push out the limits of the possible. One should look in the Index for one's family name (e.g. *Reuss*, on page 59 and then find suggestions at the pages indicated.

I have made the surprising discovery that what one might call the free-form nutty name – *Oldmouse Waltz, Cashmere Tango Obedience, Eucalyptus Yoho* – is the one and only indigenous American art form. Another contender, the totem pole, is also found in

New Guinea, and is extinct in America anyway; jazz, said to have originated in New Orleans funeral processions, derived from existing European and African elements. Some foreign names, notably English, have a poetic ring, but almost never as a result of fantasy. In an English or Chinese name of the richer sort logic underlies every element, as in a heraldic device; it's not, as with *Membrane Pickle, Odious Champagne or Fairy Clutter*, the free music of imagination.

Take one of my favourites, a timber merchant of Sandusky, Ohio, Mr *Humperdinck Fangboner*. Like a good *Times* crossword, the surprising parts join to produce an extraordinary whole. *Fangboner*, to start. Note the cutting edge, the spearhead: *Fang*. A clear warning – Don't Tread on Me. And the strength of the reinforcing *Bone*. Nothing supine or spineless there. It has the sinister force of Dickens's *Murdstone*. Then consider the sprightly yet harmonious overture: *Humperdinck*. First, the ominous *Hump*, evoking the ship of the desert . . . tracks across the shifting dunes, whining houris, glowering sheiks, petrodollars; or the hump of the hunchback, conferring good fortune on whoever touches it; or indeed the erotic sense of hump: fevered couplings of houris, of camels, of hunchbacks . . . but enough. Soon comes the sprightly grace note of *Dink*, in, as it were, *allegro spiritoso* time, with its refreshing contrast to the sombre weight of *Hump* and *Fang* – a spoonful of sherbet between two rich plates of a sumptuous banquet.

And then, like the resolution of the primary and secondary themes of a symphony, the full *Humperdinck*, suggesting musical genius, Hansel and Gretel wandering in a wood . . . so fitting for one called by destiny to deal in the products of the forest. Finally the magnificent consummation, the whole orchestra, *tutti, fortissimo*, in C major; *HUMPERDINCK FANG-BONER*. A *recondita armonia* . . . evocative as a verse of Mallarmé, a haiku of Bashò.

We find nothing comparable to these American fantasies in other cultures, except here and there in fiction. Dickens, to be sure, the Mozart of the funny names business, showed a marvellous power of onomastic invention, but it fell to the New World to plant its flag upon the heights to which he pointed the way. America, not old England, brought forth *Katz Meow, Positive Wassermann Johnson*, and *Unable To Fornicate*, just as so many of the visions of Jules Verne were finally reduced to practice by the National Aeronautics and Space Administration.

As a by-product of détente we are considering a branch in the Soviet Union. After the Revolution, optimistic comrades favoured names like *Tractor* or *Electrification*. One enthusiast called his twin daughters *Anarchy* and *Utopia*. A frequent practice was to contrive such acronyms as *Melor* (Marx-Engels-Lenin-October-Revolution). Now that the business has turned sour and become something they would rather not think about, and with even *Pravda* deploring these 'tasteless inventions', the classless parents are at a loss. Authoritative guidance will, we understand, be welcome. We shall be there, obstetrical bag packed, as always, not with forceps and chloroform, but with our trusty microfiches and thesaurus. Our preliminary approved list includes *Peaceful Coexistence* and *Virgin Lands* for girls, and for boys, *Norm*, *SAM*, and *Posthumous Rehabilitation*.

My interest in bizarre names has been accompanied by a weakness for curious episodes, what the French call *faits divers*. In college I sometimes included in my notes the literary ancedotes recounted by the lecturers. Several of the episodes in this book come from that time. European newspapers like them, and while living abroad I collected a number.

My take-off point in the bizarre occurrences business probably came in Toulouse, in 1952, en route from Spain to Italy. While having breakfast in a café, I read in the local paper – the *Dépêche*, I think – under the headline *Une Jeune Mère Allaitait un Serpent* ('Young Mother Suckles Snake'), an account of an episode in Trastevere, a poor quarter of Rome. It seemed that a woman sitting in the open had fallen asleep while nursing her baby. A snake had appeared and taken the baby's place, had silenced the infant's cries by waving its tail to distract it . . . and so on.

I showed this story with some enthusiasm to the waiter, who in the jaded manner of *garçons de café* everywhere, particularly early in the morning, seemed unimpressed. 'Ah, ça, vous savez, les ritales . . .' ('Wops . . .') he said, and wandered off, shrugging vaguely. Unsatisfied by this response, I cut the story out of the paper and put it in my pocket. On reaching Florence, I tried it again on my aunt. '*Si, si, di fatti*,' she said, 'It was in the *Nazione* and the *Corriere*. In the Italian papers they ended by saying, "This kind of thing has been happening *all too frequently* of late in Trastevere!" '

I felt better, and stowed the clipping in my wallet, where in time it was joined by others picked up along the way in travels or from reading. From this period came 'Walking Iron Mine Finally Collapses', included in the present volume. As the collection grew, I

Une jeune mère allaitait un serpent

began noting discoveries in my diaries. Finally, in 1977, I exhumed my old notes and transcribed what seemed like the best, together with others looked up in various places or that have come in from correspondents.

Suggestions for a subsequent edition, or corrections, are very welcome indeed, and can be posted to Box 157, R.D. 2, Bedford, New York. Documentation is important.

To illustrate the importance of verification, I might mention the 'snake in the Christmas tree' archetype. Mr. David Binger, a close observer of conditions in the Bedford area, told me recently of a friend of his who had a neighbour who had bought a Christmas tree and taken it home with its roots wrapped in sacking. While he took a bath his wife started to cut open the coarse wrapping. Suddenly, a snake slid out from the tangle of roots. She shrieked. The husband dashed downstairs, naked and dripping. His wife excitedly told him about the snake. He snatched up a poker and peered at the base of the tree. The family retriever, intrigued, stuck his cold nose into the man's behind. The terrified man crashed into the wall, knocking himself unconscious. An ambulance was called. When the stretcher-bearers heard what had happened, they laughed so much they dropped the victim, whose arm was broken.

I started checking this story, and pursued it upstream around Westchester County through six successive sources, each of whom assured me that it had actually happened to a friend of the person he had heard it from.

During this process, Mrs. Duncan Spencer sent in an account of a Connecticut woman who came home from shopping on a winter Saturday and noticed her husband on his back under the car performing some repair. The woman, who was of a frisky disposition, scooped up a handful of snow, adroitly zipped open his trousers, and shovelled it in. The supine form convulsed, cracking its head against the crankcase. Darkness loosened his limbs, as Homer says. The woman dashed into the house to phone the doctor. She encountered her actual husband, who mentioned that he had called in a mechanic to mend the car. Again, the ambulance comes, the stretcher-bearer howls with laughter, the patient is let fall, his arm is broken.

I finally realised that both of these tales are almost certainly mutants of *The Times'* plumber story on page 176.

So one must nail down the exact origin. In the present text, anyway, the reader will observe that I've generally given citations for the contemporary episodes, and not always for the historical ones, most of which can be found in the standard sources.

Language is the highest form of culture, and surely word origins are the most fascinating element of language. It is extraordinary to think that the terms we use every day run right back to the dawn of man, and in working their way down to us through the millennia have been scarred and altered by all the accidents of history and geography through which they have passed.

Words dwell in our minds like insects in a forest, or indeed, like the countless friendly organisms that inhabit the human body. We could scarcely exist without them. They illustrate what one might call cultural Darwinism. New words arrive – borne by conquest, commerce, or science – and supplant their predecessors. But the old words never fade entirely away. They linger faintly in the shadows, understudies hoping to be called back on stage. That is why the English language is incomparably richer in nuances than its rivals, although, since always in flux, it is less precise. Because of this, English offers an unusual challenge. There is more to understand: more words, evolving senses of those words, multiple cultural backgrounds.

People unaware of the origins of the words they use don't quite realise what they are saying. They are precluded from the mot juste. Take the word dilapidated. Coming from Latin *lapis*, 'stone', it refers to crumbling masonry. So to talk about a dilapidated overcoat, for instance, may convey interesting suggestions of falling masonry (or buttons), but is obviously weaker than to speak of a threadbare overcoat, just as speaking of a threadbare wall would be silly. I am always exasperated by references to a *library* of wine in gushy magazine articles. *Liber* means 'book', after all.

The search for word origins is complicated by interesting traps. For instance, in earlier centuries devising conjectural etymologies out of whole cloth was considered to be a legitimate activity. So Anglo-Saxon terms were blithely given fantastic Greek and Latin sources that could never have been. Only the more systematic etymology of recent generations has rooted out many of these whimsies.

The reader is warned against plausible explanations of common words on the basis of single episodes. These tales are usually wrong: e.g., accounting for *pumpernickel* as Napoleon's observation that it was *'bon pour Nickel'*, his horse,* or the *sirloin* canard, for which see page 164, or the notion that *marmalade*† was offered as a cure to Mary Queen of Scots, *Marie Malade*.

Folk-etymology is a mine field. Take the English country term for *asparagus*. Finding the name peculiar, the country folk transformed it into *sparrowgrass*, which seemed more sensible. The Far

Eastern English word *compound*, in the sense of a large enclosure, was originally Malay *kampong*. There are a number of other examples in the text, such as *hobson-jobson* and *humble pie*. ‡

Back-formation, of which an example is described under *Cambridge*, is similar.

Another curious category is ghost words, which arise from the inaccuracies of dictionary-makers. A list of them is found at the end of the *Oxford English Dictionary*. As an example the reader might consider the evolution, over five centuries, of a *business* of ferrets into a *freamyng*, described on page 184. Sometimes authors, misunderstanding older texts, invent false senses for words. Sir Walter Scott was a specialist, *derring-do* being an example. He found the word in Spenser, who, however, had got it incorrectly from Lidgate, who had in turn garbled a text of Chaucer.

Then, there is the vast field of disputed origins. Often, as with archaeology or paleontology, one is reconstructing history on the basis of fragments, which lend themselves to different interpretations. For example, while the standard sources agree that *mumbo jumbo* (see page 188) comes from the Mandingo language, some authorities aver that it means 'a witch doctor with a feather headdress', while others, equally learned, hold for 'Be off, troublesome grandmother!' One often gets the desperate feeling that there are no absolutely certain etymologies.

Welsh *rarebit*, originally the same cheese dish but called Welsh *rabbit*, typifies the category of genteel-isms. It was a modest joke, suggesting that the Welsh were so poor they ate cheese and called it rabbit. But pompous menu writers couldn't accept anything that simple, and so came up with the baseless notion of the *rarebit*.

An aspect of language that 'moderns' often don't recognise is that 'primitive' people frequently have much larger and richer vocabularies than ours, and understand them better. Indeed, literacy may, like television, enfeeble language, not enhance it. Homer didn't read or write. Travelling in the Middle East I have heard Arab intellectuals say, 'I must go and live among the Bedouins for a while and learn to speak Arabic again.' Bedouin Arabic is more generously studded with proverbial wisdom than the language of the city dwellers, corrupted by advertising lingo and the debased usage of the media. I suspect that if my grandfather, who died a century ago, returned to Earth, the three things that would surprise him most would be telecommunications, inflation, and the drastic shrinkage of our vocabulary. The rest was largely foreseen by Jules Verne.

Certainly, those who aren't conscious of the sources of their language, like those who subsist on tinned vegetables, miss a lot: the tang and aroma are gone. I hope this little book will contribute to enlivening language for the reader. As Auden said, through etymology words become brief lyrics about themselves.

—J. T.

* In fact it comes from German *pumpern*, 'fart'.
† From Portuguese *marmelada*, 'quince'.
‡ The evolution of English inn names over the centuries provide some fascinating cases: *The Infanta de Castilla* (commemorating a royal visit) into *Elephant and Castle*; *God Encompasses Us* into *Golden Compasses*; *Boulogne Mouth* (celebrating a military success) into *Bull and Mouth*; *route du roi* into *Rotten Row*.

Lotta Crap

NAMES

A. A. A. D'ARTAGNAN UMSLOPAGAAS DYNAMITE MACAULAY
(The Times)

ABDERAZZAQ S. ABDEULHAFAFEETH
Fitchburg, Massachusetts
(Fitchburg Sentinel)

AIDA QUATTLEBAUM *
Westminster, California

* *Compare Tosca Zerk, daughter of Oscar Zerk, inventor of the Zerk Auto Grease Gun.*

ANIL G. SHITOLE *
Rochester, New York

* *Compare Pupo Shytti, Vice President of Albania, Mrs. P. Shittachitta, Mililani Town, Honolulu* (Honolulu Star Bulletin)*, and Ms. Somchittindepata, Ithaca, N.Y. Dr. Sylvan Stool is a prominent Philadelphia surgeon, Lotta Crap is the daughter of Paul Crap of Crap Bakery, Greencastle, Ind., and Atholl McBean is a San Francisco social leader.*

1

AL DENTE
Policeman*
Plantation, Florida
(The Miami Herald)
* Resigned, complaining pay inadequate.

A. MORON
Commissioner of Education
Virgin Islands

ANNE AASS
Pittsburgh, Pennsylvania

APPENDICITIS, LARYNGITIS, MENINGITIS, PERITONITIS, and TONSILLITIS JACKSON
(Newsweek)

A. PRZYBYSZ*
Detroit, Michigan
** Changed his name in 1940 – to C. Przybysz (*Newsweek*).*

ARGUE & PHIBBS
Solicitors
Albert Street, Sligo, Eire

ARIZONA ZIPPER
New York City
(Village Voice)

2

ARYSTOTLE TOTTLE*
Pirate
Falmouth, England

* 'A timid pyrate.' Gosse, A History of Piracy. New York: Tudor Publishing Co., 1934.

Aristotle Tottle, a very timid feeble pyrate

ASA MINER *
Wakefield, Rhode Island

* Compare Asia, Africa, America, and Europe Hamlin. Another brother, Hannibal, Vice President of the United States 1861 to 1865, nearly lost the election for Abraham Lincoln because his brother Africa was widely assumed to be black.

ATOMIC ZAGNUT ADAMS
Son of Founder of Gesundheit Institute, Arlington, Virginia
(The Washington Post)

A. TOXEN WORM
Theatrical Press Agent
New York City

AURORA BOREALIS BELSKY *
Staten Island, New York

* Compare Vernal Equinox Grossnickel, Blanchester, Ohio.

AURORA CABANGBANG
Virginia
(Division of Vital Records and Health Statistics, Department of Health, Richmond, Virginia)

AVE MARIA KLINKENBERG
Yonkers, New York

4

Aurora Borealis Belsky

PRIVATE BABY CHERRY *
U.S. Army
(225th Quartermaster Battalion)
* *Compare Private Parts, U.S. Army, and Private Murder
Smith, British Army.*

5

BADMAN TROUBLE*
Chief Baggage Handler
Panamerican Airways
Roberts Field, Liberia

* *'He was, and gave us a lot of,' reports our correspondent.*

BAMBANG WINNEBOSO
Banker
Bank of America
Ceylon

BAMBINA BROCCOLI*
New York City

* *Compare Concerto Macaroni.*

BASIL CRAPSTER*
Princeton University (Class of 1941)
Princeton, New Jersey

* *Compare E. C. Crapp, Washington, D.C.: Gladstone P.
Lillycrap, U.S. Attorney; and Toilet Jacobs. Sharon
Willfahrt and Tunis Wind were students of the Art
Instruction School, Minneapolis, Minn.*

SIR BASIL SMALLPEICE
Chairman, Cunard Line
London, England

BATHSHEBA FINKELSTEIN
High School of Music & Art (Class of 1957)
New York City

6

B. Brooklyn Bridge
(John Hancock Life Insurance Company)

Dr. Beaver*
Obstetrician
Falls Church, Virginia

Compare Dr. Fealy, gynaecologist, West Palm Beach, Fla., Dr. Paternite, obstetrician, Akron, Ohio, and Dr. Fillerup, obstetrician, Pasadena, Ca.

Mrs. Belcher Wack Wack*

Miss Belcher married Mr. Wack twice.

Betty Burp
(Bureau of Vital Statistics, Jacksonville, Florida)

Rev. Blanco White*

A waverer. Ordained a priest in 1800; thereafter Professor of Religion. Renounced Christianity and abandoned the priesthood, 1810. Re-embraced Christianity, 1812; re-ordained, 1814 (Dictionary of National Biography). *Another Blanco White is a Divorce Commissioner in London.*

Mr. Boeras*
Registered Colon Therapist
Sarasota, Florida

The Compiler has his professional literature.

DR. BONEBRAKE
Bonebrake Chiropractic Center
Wichita, Kansas

MR. BONES
Undertaker
Glasgow, Scotland

BONNIE BEE BUZZARD *
'The Roost'
Wayland, Massachusetts

*Compare Sir Farquhar Buzzard, personal physician of
King George IV.*

THE BORING SCHOOL*
Boring, Oregon

*Compare the Cretin School, St. Paul, Minn., and the
(Gov.) Dummer School. Dr. Boring, dentist, drills away in
St. Petersburg, Fla., while the Rev. Boring soothes his flock
in the Bethel Alliance Church in Sandusky, Ohio.*

BUFORD PUSSER*
Heroic Sheriff
Selmer, Tennessee

*A suspicious car crash ended his career in 1977.
Compare Cotys Mouser, chief clerk, U.S. Senate Committee
on Agriculture and Forestry.*

BUGLESS, ENERGETIC, EUPHRATES, AND
GOLIATH SMITH*

(Indexes of Births for England and Wales)
Cited in Dunkling, First Names First. *London: J. M. Dent
and Sons, 1977.*

The Boring School

DR. BULL*
Pennsylvania State Secretary of Agriculture
Philadelphia, Pennsylvania
* *Subject of celebrated headline:* BULL TO SPEAK ON
ARTIFICIAL INSEMINATION.

MESSRS. BULL AND SCHYTT
Glaciologists
General Assembly, International Union of Geodesy
and Geophysics
Geneva, Switzerland

BUMPUS MCPHUMPUS ANGELEDES *
Virginia
(Division of Vital Records and Health Statistics,
Department of Health, Richmond, Virginia)
*Compare Bump and Twinkle Quick, brother and sister,
Silvester, Georgia.*

BUNCHA LOVE *

(Newsweek)

*Compare Felicity Pratt Love, Holy Love, and Wonderful
Love, all of New York. Miss Magnetic Love was a secretary
in the Army Air Corps. Hastie Love was convicted of rape in
Tennessee.*

BUNYAN SNIPES WOMBLE, Lawyer,
and CALDER WELLINGTON WOMBLE *
Winston-Salem, North Carolina

*'He enjoyed discussing the hyphen which in 1913 forever
linked the towns of Winston and Salem,' and for which,
indeed, as head of the Winston Consolidation Committee,
he was in large measure responsible.*

10

Buncha Love

11

ROMANTIC
ENTANGLEMENTS

Mrs. Czermak's Descent

PRAGUE – Vera Czermak jumped out of her third-storey window when she learned her husband had betrayed her.

Mrs. Czermak is recovering in hospital after landing on her husband, who was killed, the newspaper *Vercerni Pravha* reported today. – *United Press*

Speak for Yourself, Wong

TAIPEI – A young Taiwanese man has written 700 love letters to his girl friend over the past two years trying to get her to marry him.

His persistence finally brought results.

A newspaper reported yesterday the girl has become engaged to the postman who faithfully delivered all the letters. – *United Press*

Good Form

Some months after obtaining his divorce, Walter Davis of London consulted a matrimonial bureau in the hope of finding a new companion, the *Settimana Enigmistica* of Milan reported in September, 1975.

Out of thousands of names, the bureau's computer selected that of his former wife Ethel, who had

Mrs Czermak's descent

consulted the same agency, and whom Mr. Davis
obediently remarried.

Liebestodt

MARRIED: Moses Alexander, aged 93, to Mrs. Frances
Tompkins, aged 105, in Bata, N.Y., on June 11, 1831.

They were both taken out of bed dead the following morning.*

* Kentucky Marriages, 1797–1865. *Baltimore: Genealogical Publishing Company, 1966.*

Greek Drama

An Athenian took a taxi to his lady-love's house, letting himself in with a key she had given him.

After a while they were surprised *in flagrante* by the taxi driver, who had let himself in with his own key. It was his house. The lady was his wife.

Lovers Cut Free from Embrace

LONDON – A tiny sports car leaves a lot to be desired as a midnight trysting spot, two secret lovers have learned.

Wedged into a two-seater, a near-naked man was suddenly immobilized by a slipped disc, trapping his woman companion beneath him, according to a doctor writing in a medical journal here.

The desperate woman tried to summon help by honking the horn with her foot. A doctor, ambulance driver, firemen, and a group of interested passersby* quickly surrounded the car in Regent's Park

'The lady found herself trapped beneath 200 pounds of pain-racked, immobile man,' said Dr. Brian Richards of Kent.

'To free the couple, firemen had to cut away the car frame,' he said.

The distraught woman, helped out of the car and into a coat, sobbed: 'How am I going to explain to my husband what has happened to his car?' – *Reuter*

---

* *Including women volunteer workers who arrived to serve tea, the* London Sunday Mirror *reported.*

DISORDERS

Amuck

When a Malay runs *amok* he seizes his *kris* and dashes forth to hack at anyone he encounters.

Bedlam

A contraction* of *Bethlehem* from the Hospital of St. Mary of Bethlehem, a London lunatic asylum.

Bethlehem is the Hebrew *Beth-lehem*, 'House of bread'.

* *Like the shrinkage of Mary* Magdalen *into* maudlin.

Berserk

Literally, 'bear shirt'.

The Norse sagas describe a family who went into battle in a frenzy of blood lust, clad only in bearskins; by extension all furious fighters were called 'Berserkers'. Similarly, some Celts, when in a fighting rage, took off their clothes and attacked the enemy naked.

Brouhaha

From the Hebrew *barook habbah*, 'blessed-the-comer'; as in 'Blessed be he who cometh in the name of the Lord'.

Berserk

Sixes and Sevens

To end the rivalry over precedence of two City companies, the Skinners and the Merchant Taylors, King Henry VIII decreed that they would alternate.

MORE NAMES

REVEREND CANAAN BANANA
President
Zimbabwe

CARBON PETROLEUM DUBBS *
Founder, Universal Oil Products
Des Plains, Illinois
Also introduced the Japanese beetle to Bermuda.

CARDIAC ARREST DA SILVA
Municipal Tax Collector
Brazil
(Financial Times)

CARDINAL SIN
Archbishop of Manila
Philippines

CARESSE PECOR
University of Vermont (Class of 1971)
Burlington, Vermont

CARLOS RESTREPO RESTREPO RESTREPO DE
RESTREPO
Medellin, Colombia

Cardinal Sin, Archbishop of Manila

CASHMERE TANGO OBEDIENCE*
Agriculturist
Santa Cruz, California

*Compare Clarence O. Bedient, New York Times *ad salesman.*

19

CHARLES ADOLPHE FAUX-PAS BIDET *
Commissaire de Police
Paris, France

* The Sûreté's ace on Russian intrigues, Faux-Pas Bidet received heavy press coverage in the 1930s when he investigated the abduction of Gen. Kutylpov, a White Russian leader in Paris. The general was seized in the street by OGPU agents and apparently, wrapped up as merchandise, was carried on board a Soviet ship, the Spartak, *which immediately put out to sea.*

CHARLES EVERYBODYTALKSABOUT, JR.
Seattle, Washington

CHEATHAM & STEELE *
Bankers
Wallowa County, Oregon

* The Compiler has a photograph of this establishment. Compare Haddah Cheatham Wright, owner, Cheatum's Style Shoppe, Grand Island, Nebraska, and Wylie Cheatem, Attorney General of Texas. T. Swindella was charged with fraud in London Bankruptcy Court, and Robyn Banks is a teller in the First Pennsylvania Bank, Chestnut Hill, Pa. (The Philadelphia Inquirer).

CHERRI PANCAKE *
Curator, Museo Ixchel del Traje Indigena
Guatemala City, Guatemala
* Compare Golden Pancake, Marion, Ohio.

REVEREND CHRISTIAN CHURCH *
Florence, Italy
* Active in 1966 flood relief effort. Compare Christ Apostle and Conception de Jesus, both of New York City, Rev.

Cheatham & Steele, Bankers

God, of Congaree, S.C., Rev. Christ Church, of Spartanburg, S.C., and the Rev. Hosanna, United Church of Christ, Denver, Col.

CHRIST T. SERAPHIM
Judge
Milwaukee, Wisconsin

(United Press)

21

CIGAR STUBBS
Florida
(Bureau of Vital Statistics)

(MRS.) CISTERN BROTHERS*
Hog Neck, North Carolina
* *Compare Knighton Day, New York City.*

MR. CLAPP*
Venereal Disease Counselor and Lecturer
County Health Service
San Mateo, California
* *'Kept very busy indeed' by conditions in the late sixties.*

COL. CLARENCE CLAPSADDLE
U.S. Army (West Point, Class of 1940)

CLAUDE BALL*
Seattle, Washington

(Seattle Post-Intelligencer)
* *Compare Dr. Claude Organ, surgeon and director of
Boys Town, Omaha, Nebr.*

CHIEF (CLAYTON) CROOK*
Police Chief
Brunswick, Ohio
* *A different Chief (Bernard) Crooke heads the
Montgomery County, Md., police force. Narcissus Frett is
Chief Confidential Investigator, Surrogate Court of Kings
County, N.Y.*

Sir Cloudesley Shovel, Admiral, Royal Navy

SIR CLOUDSLEY SHOVEL*
Admiral, Royal Navy

*Concluding a distinguished career, he ran the fleet on the rocks (Scilly Isles) drowning 2,000 men. As they steered into danger, a seaman who knew the waters warned of their peril. Sir Cloudsley, enraged, ordered him instantly hanged. When disaster struck, Sir Cloudsley, accompanied *by his pet whippet, set off in his Admiral's barge, which sank in turn. After struggling ashore, he was done in by a peasant woman who 'coveted an emerald ring on one of his fingers, and extinguished his flickering life'. He was buried in Westminster Abbey, 'where an elaborate monument in very questionable taste was erected to his memory'* (Dictionary of National Biography). *His gallant successor Admiral Steel Bellie recovered the Nicobar Islands; Admiral The Hon. Sir Reginald Aylmer Ranfurley Plunkett-Ernle-Erle-Drax participated in the Battle of Jutland. Captain Strong Boozer commanded the Guantanamo Naval Base, but Royal Navy Shippe has opted for life ashore with the Federal Reserve System, Washington, D.C. Commander Sink, U.S.N., hails from Fort Washington, Md.*

C. MATHEWS DICK*
Social Leader
Newport, Rhode Island

* Compare Dr. Dick, urologist, of Colorado Springs, Colo., the Griesedick (beer) family of Minneapolis, and D. Biggerdick, Art Instruction School, Minneapolis. The Dick Tool Company operates in Bronxville, N.Y.

MR. COCK MARRIED MISS PRICK*
(The Times, 1963)

* Mr. Ora Jones married a Miss Ora Jones in 1941 (R. L. Ripley).

COMFORT AND SATISFY BOTTOM*
Sisters
Wayne State University
Detroit, Michigan

* Compare Silas Comfort Swallow, 1904 Prohibition

24

Party candidate for President, and Dreama Bottoms, Duke University, Durham, N.C. Also Barbara Fatt Heine, New York City (New York Times) *and Bonnie Pubus, Cambridge, Mass.*

Comfort and Satisfy Bottom, Sisters

COMMODORE DEWEY THIGPEN
Janitor
Corpus Christi, Texas

CONSTANT AGONY *
Chazy Lake, New York

Compare Agonia Heimerdinger, Santa Ana, Calif.

REV. CORNELIUS WHUR*
Trashy Poet (1782–1853)
England

An impression of the Rev. Whur's output can perhaps be conveyed by the following:

The Female Friend

In this imperfect, gloomy scene
Of complicated ill,
How rarely is a day serene,
The throbbing bosom still!
Will not a beauteous landscape bright
Or music's soothing sound,
Console the heart, afford delight,
And throw sweet peace around?
They may; but never comfort lend
Like an accomplished female friend.

With such a friend the social hour
In sweetest pleasure glides;
There is in female charms a power
Which lastingly abides;
The fragrance of the blushing rose,
Its tints and splendid hue,
Will with the season decompose,
And pass as flitting dew;
On firmer ties his joys depend
Who has a faithful female friend.

COTYS M. MOUSER
Chief Clerk, U.S. Senate
Committee on Agriculture and Forestry
Washington, D.C.

CRANBERRY TURKEY BRECKENRIDGE, JR.
Virginia
(Division of Vital Records and Health Statistics,
Department of Health, Richmond, Va.)

CRYSTAL TOOT
President, Kansas State PTA
Great Bend, Kansas

C. SHARP MINOR*
Silent Movie Organist
Rochester, New York
*Compare O. Pinkypank, ukelele instructor, Sweet
Springs, Mo.

CUMMING & GOOING
Louisiana
(New Yorker)

CUPID RASH*
England

(Western Morning News)
*Father of nine; succeeded in getting eleven years behind
in his rent before being evicted from public housing
project.

Cumming & Gooing, Louisiana

AFFAIRS OF STATE

Surtout Point de Zèle

Thomas Jefferson, speaking of the American minister to Spain: 'I haven't heard from him in two years. If I don't hear from him next year, I will write him a letter.'

Chops Populi

Victor Biaka-Boda, who represented the Ivory Coast in the French Senate,* set off on a tour of the hinterlands in January 1950 to let the people know where he stood on the issues, and to understand their concerns – one of which was apparently the food supply. His constituents ate him.

His colleagues, according to an account in Time *magazine in July 1951, remembered Biaka-Boda, a former witch doctor, as a 'small, thin, worried-looking man'.*

The Career of the Vasa

Gustavus II Adolphus, king of Sweden, troubled by Hapsburg pressure on the Baltic, commanded that the mightiest warship on any ocean be constructed as the flagship of his navy. Designed to carry 500 sailors and troops, she was named the *Vasa*, after his own dynasty.

Finally, her powerful armaments, her stout rigging, her splendid ornamentation, were complete.

On Sunday, August 10, 1628, Captain Söfring

Hanson gave the order to sail. High court and military dignitaries were on board. A throng lined the Stockholm waterfront to admire the magnificent vessel and enjoy the soft light of the summer afternoon.

Warped along the quays of the Skeppsbron, her figurehead, a nobly carved and gilded lion, turned its

The career of the Vasa

grave face out into the bay. A gentle breeze from the heights of Söder filled the acres of white canvas.

The ship gained way slowly. She fired the two-gun salute of departure.

The wind picked up and the *Vasa* heeled, farther, farther . . .

Suddenly the sea poured into the open gunports, only a yard above the waterline.

With a deep, melancholy crashing and pounding as the munitions and stores shifted in the hold, the huge vessel heeled more sharply. The rail entered the water; the waves lapped over the deck. The hull slid into the depths. Masts and sails slowly vanished. Finally, the last pennant, bravely waving still, disappeared into the pale blue Baltic.*

* *Cf. Bengt Ohrelius,* Vasa: The King's Ship. *New York: Chilton Books, 1962.*

Protocol

American Ambassador Joseph Hodges Choate was leaving an official reception in London, dressed in plain black, America having no diplomatic uniform. Another ambassador, mistaking him for a servant, briskly commanded, 'Call me a cab!'

Choate gazed at him a moment, and then replied genially, 'You're a cab, sir.'*

* *Choate, according to his family, later told the enraged diplomat, 'If you'd been better looking, I would have called you a* hansom *cab.'*

A Diplomatic Reception

The first European ever seen in Sikkim was Deputy Commissioner Campbell of Darjeeling. He toiled his way up in the time of the great-grandfather of the present Chogyal.*

Campbell's materialization in the audience room dismayed His Highness.

CHOGYAL (*to his vizier, the only English-speaking courtier*): Who are these extraordinary creatures with red faces and hair growing out of their cheeks? They look like monkeys!

VIZIER (*blandly, bowing to Deputy Commissioner Campbell*): His Highness bids you welcome. He expresses the hope that your journey was not unduly arduous.

* *Who told me the story in 1968.*

LOVE

Boudoir

From the French *bouder*, 'pout'. So a *boudoir* is a

Boudoir

room where madame can go and sulk.* A lady can also do so in her *sulky*: a carriage for one.

And where she might say to herself, 'Je m'en fous comme de l'an quarante.' The French use this strange phrase, which means literally 'I don't care any more about it than for the year 40', in the sense of 'I couldn't care less.'

It apparently survives from a Crusader's expression, Je m'en fous comme de l'al-Koran, 'I don't care any more about it than for the Koran.'

Bridal

A *bridal* party is expected to drink a lot. The word comes from the Old English 'bride-ale' that was drunk at marriages before champagne became the rule.

A *buxom* bride should love, honour, and above all obey, since the word originally meant 'pliant' or 'obedient'.

Her consort was formerly the *goom* or 'man'. He was later (and somewhat insultingly) reduced to a mere stableboy – *groom* – by folk-etymology.

Bugger

The Cathari, a Bulgarian heretical sect of the Middle Ages, believed in eliminating sin by letting humanity die out through abstention from sex.

They were, inevitably, reproached for sodomy. Persons of that tendency came to be called 'Bulgars': Latin *Bulgarus*, French *bougre*, English *bugger*.

Catamite

The passive partner among two male homosexuals. The word has evolved over countless centuries from

Ganymede (son of King Tros of Troy), whom Zeus carried off to be his cupbearer and sex object, and whom the Romans called *Catamitus*.

Flirt

Flirt started out from Italy long ago referring to

Flirt

flowers, and reappeared there from England as a romantic euphemism.

Italian picture magazines like to print breathless accounts of the latest Riviera playboy *'passando un idillio con la sua ultimissima flirt',* pronounced 'fleert'. They consider this delicate expression for 'mistress' quite English but in fact it comes from the French *fleureter*, and ultimately from Italian *fiorare*, to 'throw bouquets' of compliments.

The idea is echoed in the Spanish expression for making flattering comments to a passing girl: *echar flores*, to 'throw flowers'.

Miniature

The miniature of her loved one in a lady's locket originally referred not to its size but to the kind of paint.

The brilliant red colour monks used in decorating medieval manuscripts was called minium (red lead) in Latin, and that art was called *miniating*. A picture illuminating the text – necessarily small because of the limited space available – was thus called a *miniature*.

Perfume

A woman's *perfume* derives from Latin *fumus*, 'smoke': the smoke or incense arising from a burning sacrifice* in ancient religion.

*A holocaust *is an 'entirely burnt' sacrifice.*

NAMES AGAIN

DAPHNE READER'S DIGEST TAIONE
Utui, Vavao, Tonga

DR. DEADMAN*
Pathologist
Ontario, Canada

*Compare Mr. Deadman, F.B.I. analyst in trial of
murderer of 28 young blacks in Atlanta, Georgia.

DEFRED GOO FOLTS
Director of Placement
Harvard Graduate School of Business Administration
Cambridge, Massachusetts

DEMETRUS PLICK
Interior Designer
Boston, Massachusetts

(Harvard Medical School *Alumni Bulletin*)

DEMETRIUS TOODLES
Public School 92M
New York City

DENNIS ELBOW
Fisherman
Warsaw, New York
(Orvis News)

Demetrus Plick, Interior Designer

DOCTOR DOTTI*
Psychiatrist
Rome, Italy

*Once husband of Audrey Hepburn. Compare Dr.
Dement, psychiatrist, Stanford University, and Jean
Wierdo, mental patient, New Jersey State Hospital at
Greystone Park.*

DOOLITTLE & DALLEY
Estate Agents
Kidderminster, England

DR. & DR. DOCTOR*·
Westport, Connecticut

One M.D. married another. There were, by recent count, 13 doctors Doctor, Doctor, or Doktor in the U.S.; 5 doctors Bonebreak; 1 Bonecutter; 18 Butchers; several Cutters and Carvers; 184 Paines or Paynes and 11 Pangs. Dr. Bonesetter practises in Bombay, and Dr. Screech in Victoria, British Columbia. For Dr. Ovary, gynaecologist, vide infra. Among the Mormons, the seventh son of a seventh son may be named Doctor. W. Doctor Dollar, New York, has not yet entered the profession, but should. Dr. Falces (pron. 'falsies') performs breast implants at St. Luke's Hospital, San Francisco.

D. SCHUMUK*
Political Activist
Ukraine, U.S.S.R.

(Reuters)

A loser. Served 7 years in jail (prewar) for communism. Then (postwar) served 20 years and in 1972 started an additional 10 years plus 5 years exile, all for anti-communism.

EARLESS ROMERO
Lafayette, Louisiana
(Courthouse Records)

EASTER BUGGAGE*
New Orleans, Louisiana

* Offspring of Halloween Buggage. Compare Luscious Easter, Euclid, Ohio, one of the first blacks to play for the Cleveland Indians. A 'big, fence-busting first baseman', recalled Time *magazine.*

D. Schumuk, Political Activist, Ukraine

ECSTACY GOON
(Wisconsin Historical Society,
Madison, Wisconsin)

SIR EDWARD PINE-COFFIN
Poor Relief Commissioner *
Dublin, Ireland
*During the 1844–5 potato famine.

EPAPHRODITUS MARSH
ONESIPHORUS MARSH and
(ARCHBISHOP) NARCISSUS MARSH
(New York Times)

E. PLURIBUS EUBANKS *
Longshoreman
San Francisco, California
* Compare E. Pluribus Gass, Western Reserve University,
Cleveland, Ohio.

EUCALYPTUS YOHO
Ashland Oil Dealer
Portsmouth, Ohio

EVAN KEEL
Goldsboro, North Carolina

EVE I. WARMFLASH
Class of 1980
Clark University
Worcester, Massachusetts

E. Z. MILLION
Director
Southwest Computer Conference
Tulsa, Oklahoma

FAIR HOOKER
Football Player (End), for the Cleveland Browns
Cleveland, Ohio

FAIRY CLUTTER
Indiana University of Pennsylvania Women's Club
Indiana, Pennsylvania

DR. FANG *
Dentist
Tillman Clinic
Belmont, Massachusetts

Dr. Gargle, New York City dentist, has now retired to Florida. Dr. Toothaker, a dentist with the Arizona Public Health Service, was killed by a rock fall while visiting the Navajo National Monument. Dr. E. Z. Filler practices dentistry in Roslyn Heights, N.Y., Dr. Pull in St. Cloud, Minn., Dr. Warmflash in Stamford, Conn., Dr. Pulls at St. Mark's clinic, New York City, and Dr. Screech in Essex, England.

FANG W. WANG
Mutual Fund Executive
New York City

FANNY FINGER*
New York City

*Compare Hyman Peckeroff, taxi driver, New York City;
and Hyman Pleasure, Assistant Commissioner, New York
State Department of Mental Hygiene.*

FANNY HUNNYBUN*
Nanny
South Devon, England

*Met and married Mr. Hunnybun, guest of employer.
Died in 1975, aged 97.*

FARTINA GREENE
Virginia
(Division of Vital Records and Health Statistics,
Department of Health, Richmond, Virginia)

FAUNTLEROY SCHNAUZ
(Educational Testing Service
Princeton, New Jersey)

FEMALE JONES*
University of Maryland Hospital
Baltimore, Maryland

*This not unusual given name – bestowed by hospitals in
the absence of a parental decision – is often pronounced
fe-mà-le. Compare Legitimate Jones and Male Infant
Kilgore, both of Detroit, Mich.*

F. G. VERENESENECKOCKKROCKOFF*
San Francisco, California

*Defendant in a celebrated murder trial in 1897.
See Jennings, Personalities of Language.
London: Gollancz, 1967.*

Felonious Fish

FIRMIN A. GRYP*
Banker
Northern California Savings & Loan Association
Palo Alto, California

** Compare Mr. Overcash, President, American Credit
Corporation, Dallas, Texas.*

(MISS) FISHY STEP*
Pennsylvania

Arrested for vagrancy. Compare Felonious Fish, Omaha, Nebraska, Halibut Justa Fish, Mastic, N.Y., and Fish Fish (London News Chronicle).

FORTUNATE TARTE
Mary Fletcher Hospital,
Burlington, Vermont

REV. FOUNTAIN WETMORE RAINWATER*
Circuit-riding Preacher
Kentucky

Liked to sprint to church, read one verse from the Bible, and sprint home. Compare Judith Moist.

(MADAME) FOUQUEAU DE PUSSY*
Authoress

Le Grand-pere et ses quatre petits fils. Boston: Hickling, Swan and Brown, 1855. Compare Graze Pussy, New York City, and Grace Marie Antoinette Jeanne d'Arc de Repentigny, maiden name of Grace Metalious, trashy novelist.

BRIGADIER FRIED BURGER
Commander, Royal Brunei Malay Regiment
Brunei

MRS. FRIENDLY LEY*
Mission Hills, California

On whose career of amiability the curtain descended when her husband's revolver, which he was cleaning in the kitchen, went off.

Madame Fouqueau de Pussy, Authoress

FUZZEY TELEVISION, LTD.*
St. Peter Port, Guernsey, Channel Islands
* Establishment patronised by the Compiler.

46

Mrs Friendly Ley, Mission Hills, California.

UNBALANCED DIETS

Walking Iron Mine Finally Collapses

TOBATA, JAPAN – A bet made several years ago finally

Walking iron mine

caught up with 51-year-old Otoichi Kawakami last night.

Mr. Kawakami had convulsions and fainted in downtown Tobata. He was rushed to a hospital where surgeons removed from his stomach 13 safety razors complete with blades, 21 nails, a fountain pen, a pencil, 56 toothbrushes, 20 chopsticks, a piece of wire netting, and part of the ribs of an umbrella. He said he swallowed the assortment on a bet several years ago. – *United Press*

Rupture of the Deep

A group of city dignitaries staged a festivity to celebrate the joining of the two shafts of a tunnel under a river. The party, which Sir Robert Davis, an authority on diving, described to Jacques Cousteau, took place down in the tunnel.

The dignitaries cheerfully drank a quantity of champagne. It tasted flat: since the tunnel was under pressure, the carbon dioxide bubbles were held in solution.

When the city fathers were hoisted to the surface the carbon dioxide in their stomachs erupted. They blew up like bullfrogs and had to be lowered hastily back into the tunnel again.*

* *Cf. Jacques Cousteau,* The Silent World. *New York: Harper and Row, 1953.*

Higher Education

American college students of the '50s and '60s enjoyed swallowing whole schools of goldfish. They also practised crowding into telephone booths (the record was 31 in one booth) and they liked to destroy pianos. Two Delta Chi members tore one apart, passing the fragments through a 9-inch ring, in 4 minutes and 51 seconds at Wayne State University, Detroit.

Contretemps

Victorien Sardou, the French playwright and *salon* figure, knocked over his wine glass at a dinner party. The lady next to him sprinkled salt on the stain. Sardou tossed some over his shoulder to ward off ill fortune, straight into the eyes of a waiter who was about to serve him chicken. The man clutched his eyes and the platter crashed to the floor.

The family dog, rising from his post by the fire, attacked the fowl so greedily that he began to choke.

The son of the house jumped up to wrestle the bone out of the dog's throat. The dog savagely bit the son's finger. It had to be amputated.

Eating Democrats

Alferd Packer ate five prospectors whom he was guiding over a high Colorado plateau in 1874.

The judge who sentenced Packer to hang indignantly pointed out that 'There was only six Democrats in all of Hinsdale County and you ate five of them.'*

The Department of Agriculture startled the official community by dedicating the cafeteria in its Washington building to Alferd Packer in 1977. The General Services Administration then removed the dedicatory plaque, accusing the Department of Agriculture of 'bad taste'.

JOB DESCRIPTIONS

Admiral

From the Arabic *amir-al-bahr*, 'lord (or king) of the sea'. The *d* may have crept in by association with 'admire'.*

* Admiral King, who led the U.S. Navy in World War II, was thus literally 'King of the King', and Columbus, whose Spanish title was 'Admiral of the Ocean Sea', becomes 'King of the Sea Sea Sea'. The title of Admiral returned to Arabic, as described in Ibn Khaldoun's Prolegomena, *thus becoming a Grand Tour Word: cf. page 185.*

Assassin

In the 11th and 12th centuries, the *Hashashin* ('hashish eaters') were a secret murder cult of the Ismaili sect of Muslims, followers of the Old Man of the Mountain, Hasan ben Sabah. Originally based at Alamut, south of the Caspian, they spread and became feared throughout Islam.

Marco Polo describes the Old Man offering his followers sensual pleasures including beautiful maidens, music, and hashish, so that they supposed they were in heaven. He then sent them forth on gangland-style missions to rub out prominent targets, assuring them of a quick trip to paradise if things went sour. (One of the 'hashish eaters' stabbed Edward Longshanks at the battle of Acre.)

In 1252 they were broken by the Tartars under Alaü, their fortress levelled, and the Old Man put to death. The *Hashashin* survived in our word *assassin*.

Chauffeur

French for a 'heater'. Originally this term was used for a particularly nasty breed of robbers, who broke into houses, seized the occupants, and then tortured them by burning their feet in the fireplace until they disclosed where they had stashed their valuables.

Later, the word was applied to stokers of steam engines, including the early automobiles, which ran on steam.

Finally, *chauffeur* came to mean the driver of any car.

Diplomat

Greek for 'folded twice'. A diplomat dealt in matters so secret that the documents required this special precaution.

Hooker

This American synonym for prostitute memorialises certain ladies associated with Civil War General Hooker, whose headquarters were decribed as 'half bar-room, half brothel'.

Lord

In Old English the head of the house was called the *hlaf-weard*: 'loaf warden', or 'master of the bread'. This approached the 1960s use of 'bread' for 'money', or, indeed, the biblical 'daily bread'.

On the way to *lord* it passed through many intermediate forms such as *hlaford* and *louerd*.

Similarly, a *lady* was originally the 'bread-kneader', *hlaefdige*, before becoming *levedi, levdi*, and finally, in the 14th century, *ladi*.

A retainer, in Old English, is a *hlafeta*, 'bread-eater'.

Pontiff

Pontiff comes from the Latin *pontifex*, 'bridge-builder'. Once a year in ancient Rome the *pontiffs*, led by their chief, the *pontifex maximus*, or 'chief bridge-builder', solemnly threw 23 straw dolls called *argei* into the Tiber. This was to compensate the river-god for the drowned travellers he had forgone as solid bridges replaced leaky rowboats.

With time, the Pope succeeded to the title: in English, Supreme Pontiff. In recent years, however, he has neglected to throw the dolls into the river.

Postman

The term *post* to describe messenger relay stations originated in the 13th century with Marco Polo. He described Kublai Khan's network of more than 10,000 *yambs*, or relay stations, calling them, in Italian, *poste*, or 'posts'. They were located every 25 to 45 miles on the principal roads throughout the empire. In addition, at 3-mile intervals between the *poste* there were relay stations for runners, who in lieu of the sirens we would use today wore wide belts with bells on them to signal the importance of their business.

Posting in the sense of rising to the motion of a horse's trot also comes ultimately from Marco Polo's expression, as do *postilion,** *posthaste*, *postage*, and *postman*.

* *My favourite expression from a foreign language phrase book is: 'Great heavens, the postilion has been struck by lightning.'*

FURTHER NAMES

BARONESS GABY VON BAGGE OF BOO
(New York Times)

GARNISH LURCH*
Railway Engineer
Jamaica Government Railways
Jamaica

** At the throttle when a derailment killed 178 excursionists
and injured several hundred more (*The Daily Gleaner,
1957, Kingston, Jamaica).*

GENGHIS COHEN*
Student
Orewa, Rodney County, New Zealand

* Probably the only listing to be half Maori and half Jewish.

GEORGE BARETITS
U.S. Army

GINGER SCREWS CASANOVA*
Eureka, California

(Eureka Times-Standard)

* Compare Mutual Screw Company, New York City.

Goody P. Creep, Undertaker

GISELLA WERBEZIRK-PIFFL*
Actress
Vienna and Hollywood

** Perennial victim of prewar Hollywood jokers who liked
to telephone from poolside to ask if she was the Gisella
Werbezirk-Piffl they had met in (e.g.) Monte Carlo the
previous summer; on receiving assurance to the contrary*

they would pronounce grandly, 'Ah! Then that must have been another *Gisella Werbezirk-Piffl!' Compare Josette Legg Snowball (Actress, D'Oyly Carte Company).*

GLASSCOCK VERSUS BALLS
Much-cited mortgage case
(24 Q.B.D. 13, 6 T.L.R. 57)

GORILLA HARISON *
Virginia
(Division of Vital Records and Health Statistics,
Department of Health, Richmond, Va.)
* Female (born 1924).

GRECIAN T. SNOOZE *
Australian University Student (Class of 1950)
* Dunkling, op. cit.

GRETEL VON GARLIC *
New York City
* Compare Ginger Clam, New York City.

GROANER DIGGER *
Undertaker
Houston, Texas

(Today's Health)

* Compare Goody P. Creep, Undertaker. A Mr. Bones is an undertaker in Glasgow, Scotland, Will Plant in Mumbles, Swansea, Wales, and J. Posthumus in Grand Rapids, Mich. (Playboy). The Quick-Park Funeral Home was for many years at 617 Columbus Avenue, Sandusky, Ohio. The Wing On Funeral Home is found in Toronto, the Mole Funeral Home in Barnwell, Ga., and Human & Pitt Funeral Services in Praetoria, South Africa.

HADASSAH PECKER
Physician
New York City

HALLOWEEN BUGGAGE
The Charity Hospital
New Orleans, Louisiana

HANNIBAL TOTO *
Rome, Italy
(Daily Mail)

** At a wedding, was requested to fire a salute; complied,
using a shotgun, wounding the groom and twelve of the
wedding guests. Compare A. 'Tony' Toto, pizza-maker of
Allentown, Pennsylvania, who was shot in the head by his
wife and others, then drugged, and two days later shot
again in the chest. He survived, and furnished bail to
release his wife from prison, saying, 'In my opinion it was
lack of communication – a big lack of communication.'*
(Associated Press).

HARDON COX *
Virginia
(Division of Vital Records and Health Statistics,
Department of Health, Richmond, Va.)
* Compare Adora Cox, Crapo, Md.

MR. HEADLINE *
News Director, CBS News
Washington, D.C.
** Announced plans to provide bullet-proof vests to camera
crews covering President.*

58

HECTOR SPECTOR*
Royal Canadian Air Force

Compare Hubert Boobert, trombonist, Marion, Ohio, and Esther Pester.

HEDDA HARE
Spring Valley, New York

HEIDI YUM-YUM GLUCK*
Artist
New York City

Known to the Compiler. Mr. Gluck père, infatuated by Gilbert and Sullivan, named his son Nanka, after Nanki-Poo, another character from The Mikado.

PRINCE HEINRICH THE 74TH OF REUSS*
Jankendorf, Germany
(Almanach de Gotha)

Since 1693 all males in this ancient family have been named Heinrich.

HENRY FORD CARR*
Central City, Kentucky

Compare Iona Ford and (Mr.) Zeus Garage, industrial designer.

HENRY WILL BURST
(The Times Literary Supplement)

HEINRICH LXXIV

Prince Heinrich the Seventy-Fourth of Reuss, Thuringia, Germany

HERMAN SHERMAN BERMAN *
Commissioner of Deeds
Bronx, New York

* Compare Wong Bong Fong of Hong Kong (Philadelphia Inquirer).

HILARIUS FUCHS*
Continental Grain Company
New York City
Compare Hilarious Conception, Hawaii.

Hilarius Fuchs, Continental grain Company

HOGJAW TWADDLE*
Morris Harvey College
(now University of Charleston)
Charleston, West Virginia

*Has found his name a valuable aid in breaking the ice
with new acquaintances. Compare Sianah E. Twaddle,
San Mateo, Calif.*

HONOR ROLL*
Nurse-anaesthetist
Birmingham, Alabama

Compare Charity Ball, Wichita, Kans. (Wichita Eagle).

HORACE AND BORIS MOROS*
Brothers

*Respectively, a New York City official and a Hollywood,
Calif., communist.*

HORACINE CLUTCH
Pelham, New York

E. HORRY FROST*
Incorporator, Safeway Stores
Baltimore, Maryland

*Compare (Miss) Icy Hoar, Department of Defense,
Washington, D.C.*

(MISS) HORSEY DE HORSEY
Intimate friend of Lord Cardigan*

*Who on a notable occasion banged on her door,
shouting, 'My dearest, she's dead!' – referring to her late
Ladyship – 'Let's get married at once!' Compare The*

Miss Horsey de Horsey

Honorable Outerbridge Horsey, U.S. Ambassador to Czechoslovakia.

HROTHGAR HABAKKUK
Vice-Chancellor, Oxford University

63

HUGH PUGH
Landscape Architect
London, England

Hugh Pugh, Landscape Architect, London

HUMPERDINK FANGBONER*
Lumber Dealer, and
FANNY FANGBONER
Nurse
Sandusky, Ohio

Folks in Sandusky, as in some towns in Oklahoma, seem to feel better having odd names. Other citizens of the area include Ovid Futch, Xenophon Hassenpflug, Kitty Ditty, and (from the Sandusky Register) E. Kickapoo Banfill, Lecturer.

HYMEN & COX*
Opticians
Cambridge, England

Compare Hyman Peckeroff, taxi driver, New York City (known to the Compiler); Hyman Pleasure, Assistant Commissioner, New York Department of Mental Hygiene; and Buster Hymen (San Francisco Examiner).

65

HIGH LIFE

The Mould of Form

Beau Brummel kept a special man to make only the thumbs of his gloves.

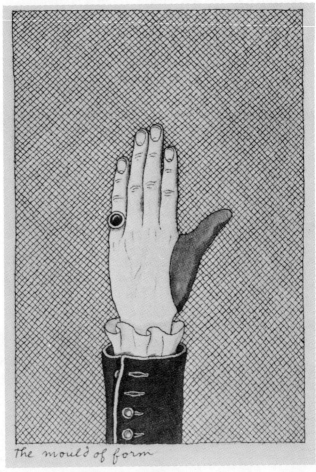

The mould of form

Clubland

The Secretary of the Atheneum, London, relates that a noble member, exasperated by slow service in the dining-room, finally asked his waiter indignantly, 'Do you know who I am?'

The waiter, contemplating the member with sympathetic concern, replied, 'No, sir. But I shall make inquiries and inform you directly.'

Alien Porn

Madame de Maintenon, wife of Louis XIV, had herself bled twice a week so that she would not blush at the salacious tales recounted by her courtiers.

Trinkets

Moulay Ismael (Sultan of Morocco 1672–1727) used to send specimens of his bowel movements to court ladies as marks of special favour.*

* *Visitors were impressed by his adroitness in mounting his horse. Sword in hand, he would leap into the saddle and simultaneously decapitate the slave who held his stirrup. It is estimated that he killed thirty thousand men with his own hand.*
  Cf. John Gunther, Inside Africa. *New York: Harper & Row, 1955.*

Bobo Decides

'Lord Salisbury . . . asked me for the weekend to his country seat, Hatfield House. On a Friday afternoon I drew up before the ancient pile, built by Salisbury's ancestor, Sir Robert Cecil, first minister to Queen Elizabeth and James I.

'I paid off the taxi and timidly rang a doorbell. To

my surprise, Lady Salisbury, a gray-haired lady with a strong ancestral face, answered the bell. With her was an enormous hound, which looked at me in a markedly unfriendly fashion and growled . . .

'Lady Salisbury . . . saw that I was nervous. "Don't worry," she said. "Bobo never bites a gentleman, only tradesmen and the lower classes."

Madame de Maintenon and friends

'At this point, Bobo lunged forward and planted his teeth in my right calf.'*

* *Stewart Alsop,* Stay of Execution. *New York: J. B. Lippincott Company, 1973.*

Trinkets

PERSONS & PLACES

Arthur

Recent research at Occidental College in California indicates that this quintessentially English hero was actually Artorius, the leader of a Sarmatian band captured by the Romans under Marcus Aurelius in the steppes of Southern Russia during the 2nd century A.D. He was re-established, with his followers, in Northern Britain. The legends they brought with them included tales suggestive of the search for the Holy Grail, with similar cup and sword symbolism.

Bistro

From the Russian *bweestra*, 'quickly!' It was a favourite command of Russian soldiers in Paris cafés after the fall of Napoleon.

Cambridge

The name of this English university town did not, as one would expect, originally refer to a *bridge* over the *Cam*, which runs through it.

The river's ancient name (by which part of it is still known) was the *Granta*, and the older name for Cambridge was *Grantacester*,* meaning a fortified Roman camp (*castra*) on the Granta.

Later it became *Grentbrigseyre, Cantbrigge*, and eventually *Cambridge*.

Finally, the river's name was changed, by what is called back-formation, to the *Cam*, to match the name of the town.

Near Cambridge lies the village of Grantchester, celebrated in Rupert Brooke's poems; the name was frozen at that point in its evolution.

Club

Men's hair gathered at the back of the head was once said to be 'clubbed', because its shape suggested a cudgel.

Habitual patrons of a coffeehouse sometimes banded together to buy the establishment when its old owner died, then installing a new manager and giving it his name: Brooks's Club, White's Club, or whatever. The term *club* was used for this arrangement by analogy to the many strands being brought together in a man's clubbed hair.

Cologne

Originally 'the colony' – *Colonia Claudia Agrippinensis.* *

* *Similarly,* Augsburg *comes from* Augustus, *and* Koblenz *from the Emperor Constantius Chlorus.*

Frank

The Franks were a Germanic tribe called by the Romans the *Franci*, after their preferred weapon, the *francus* or javelin. With the erosion of Roman power, the Franks conquered western France down to the Pyrenees. *Franc*, in Old French, came to mean 'noble' or 'free' (since the Franks had subjugated everyone else) and the word came to imply the virtues of free men: integrity and openness as opposed to the sly obsequiousness of the servile character. A *franklin* was a 'freeman' or 'freeholder'.

In Persian, Arabic, Hindi, and other languages all foreigners are called Franks; * the word also gives us *lingua franca* and *franchise*.

Frankfort, 'the ford (river-crossing) of the Franks', gave us the *frankfurter*.

Gallery

Literally, 'place of the goys'. It comes from Italian *galleria*, which comes from Medieval Latin *galeria*, apparently a variant of *galilaea*, the porch of a church (sometimes called in English a *galilee* porch).

Galilaea – or Galilee – in turn comes from the Hebrew *galil hagoyim*: 'district of the *goys* (unbelievers)'.

Kaplan

According to tradition, a 4th century Hungarian soldier, Martin, divided his cloak, or *cappella*, with his sword and gave half of it to a beggar.

After leaving the army he became a professional exorcist, and then retired to a monastery. Thereafter, he was chosen to be bishop of Tours. Eventually he rose to become patron saint of Buenos Aires, as well as of innkeepers and vine-pruners.

The half of his cloak that he had kept became an object of veneration after his death; its shrine or sanctuary thus became known as *cappella* (*Kapelle* in German, *chapelle* in French, *chapel* in English). The custodians of the shrine were for centuries known as *kapellani*.

In a surprising climax to this sequence, when German Jews of the high Middle Ages changed their names to be less conspicuous, families called *Cohen* (priest) often 'Germanized' that name into *Kaplan* (chaplain).

Kaplan

Minaret

Nur in Semitic languages means 'light'. Hebrew *menorah* thus means a 'holder of light' or 'candelabrum', and Arabic *manarah* means 'lighthouse'. The Turks used that word for the slender tower next to a mosque, which they felt had features in common with a lighthouse.

Piccaninny

From the Spanish *pequeño niño*, 'little child'.

YET MORE NAMES

ICCOLO MICCOLO
Piccolo Player
San Francisco Symphony

I. C. SHIVERS*
Iceman
(John Hancock Life Insurance Company)

* Compare Bluey Cole Snow, another John Hancock policyholder, and Norman Icenoggle (Associated Press).

IF-JESUS-CHRIST-HAD-NOT-DIED-FOR-THEE-THOU-HADST-BEEN-DAMNED BAREBONES*
London, England

* Set up the first fire insurance office in Britain. Changed his name to Nicholas Barbon. Compare Shun Fornication Barebones, N.H., and Through Trial And Tribulation We Come At Last To Heaven Slappe (London News Chronicle).

IGNATZ DANGLE
Grand Rapids Hospital,
Grand Rapids, Michigan

ILONA SCHRECK-PUROLA*
Skin Pathologist
(*Club* magazine)

* Co-authoress, Baldness and Its Cure.

IMA HOGG*
Social Leader
Houston, Texas

*Ura Hogg is a myth, but Ima June Bugg is a daughter of
the Administrator of the Farmington (Mo.) State Mental
Hospital.

IMMACULATE CONCEPTION FINKELSTEIN*
New York Stock Exchange Investor

*South American customer of Oppenheimer & Co., New
York City. Compare Modest Newcomer Weisenburg,
University of California, Berkeley, Calif.

I. M. ZAMOST
Lawyer
Highland Park, New Jersey

INGEBORG VON ZITZEWITZ*
New York City
*Known to the Compiler.

IONA VICTORY BOND
Victoria, British Columbia

I. O. SILVER
Doctor
Hazel Crest, Illinois

I. P. FRILLI*
Master Mechanic
Florence, Italy

77

Ingeborg von Zitzewitz

IRIS FAIRCLOTH BLITCH
Congresswoman
Washington, D.C.

ISRAEL GESUNDHEIT
Bankruptcy petitioner
Seattle, Washington

IVA ODOR*
Schoolteacher
Spencer, Iowa
*Compare Rev. Ivan Odor, Owosso, Mich.

IVAN KARAMANOV*

(*Maclean's* magazine)

*Changed his name to John Dinkof Doikof. Pothuvilage
Babyhamy changed her name in April 1974 to Ramya
Briget Pothuvilage.*

SIR JAMSETJEE JEJEEBHOY, 7th Bt.*

*'Son of Rustamjee J. C. Jamsetjee Jejeebhoy and Soonabai
Rustomjee Byramjee Jeejeebhoy. Succeeded cousin, Sir
Jamsetjee Jejeebhoy 6th Bt., and assumed name of
Jamsetjee Jejeebhoy in lieu of Maneckjee Rustomjee
Jamsetjee Jejeebhoy. Chairman, Sir Jamsetjee Jejeebhoy
Charity Funds, Sir Jamsetjee Jejeebhoy Parsee Benevolent
Institution; Trustee, Sir Jamsetjee Jejeebhoy School of Arts,
Byramjee Jejeebhoy Parsee Benevolent Institution. Heir,
Rustom Jejeebhoy'* (Who's Who).

MR. JOCKITCH MARRIED MISS GRUBB*
Cuernavaca, Mexico
(Park Avenue Social Review)

*Known to the Compiler. Miss Rosie Rottencrotch studied
dramatics at San Jose State University, San Jose, Calif.*

J. MINOR WISDOM*
Judge

(New York Times)

* Compare Judge Judge, Second Judicial District, State of New York. Another Judge Judge sits on the Second Circuit District Court of Maui, Hawaii.

JOHN HODGE OPERA HOUSE CENTENNIAL GARGLING OIL SAMUEL J. TILDEN TEN BROOK*
Olcott, New York

* Born in 1876, the centennial year, and named in honour of John Hodge, who owned the Hodge Opera House, manufactured gargling oil, and supported the Presidential candidacy of Samuel J. Tilden. His friends called him 'Buck'. Compare Aldeberontophoscophonia Smith, Boston, Mass., and Pepsi Cola Atom-Bomb Washington, Upper Marlboro, Md. (youngest of twenty-two children); also Third Term Roosevelt Harris (Dept. of Health, Richmond, Va.)

JOHN SENIOR, JUNIOR
New York City

JOHN WELLBORN WALLOP*
University of California
Berkeley, California
* Compare H. Wellborn Person.

JOY BANG*
Actress
New York City
* Compare Joy Hooker, Superior, Wis. (sister of Gay Hooker).

MR. JOYNT
Marijuana Analyst
Royal Canadian Mounted Police Crime Lab.
Alberta, Canada
(Christopher Logue, True Stories, *London: A. P. Rushton,
1973.)*

JULY AUGUST SEPTEMBER
(Today's Health)

JUSTIN TUNE *
Chorister
Westminster Choir College (Class of 1947)
Princeton, New Jersey
* *Compare Melody Medley, Corpus Christi, Tex., and
Melody F. Sharp, children's choir director, Salem, Va.*
*(*Associated Press*).*

KATZ MEOW
Hoquiam, Washington
(Collier's)

KATZ PAJAMA COMPANY *
New York City
* *Compare Climax Underwear Co., Cincinnati, O.*

KRAPP PERFUMERY *
Marburg, West Germany
* *The Compiler has a photograph of this establishment.*

KUHL BRIEZE
Palm Harbor, Florida

81

Katz Meow, Hoquiam, Washington

Kuhl Brieze

MEDICINE

Saving Mrs. Whitehead

Mrs. Anna C. Whitehead of Nashville, Tennessee, was felled by a drunken driver, reported the *Nashville*

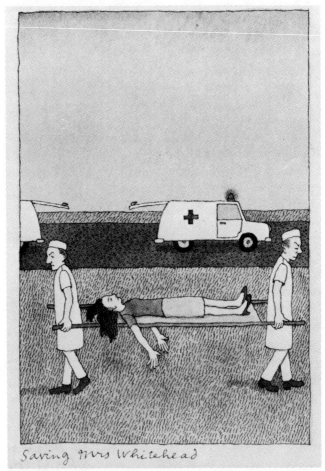

Saving Mrs Whitehead

Tennessean in January 1964. An ambulance was summoned from the Madison Funeral Home, but two other ambulances screamed first to the scene. The attendants leaped out and began to shout and struggle over the unconscious form, hauling it furiously back and forth while striking at one another. The police finally separated the combatants. Mrs. Whitehead was awarded to the original ambulance.*

* *This strange scene recalls the tug-of-war at the funeral of Verlaine in 1896 between his publisher and his mistress over possession of the winding-sheet. (During which, incidentally, a second-rate figure called Louis Aï stole fourteen of the mourners' umbrellas that had been left leaning against a tree.)*

Mars and Venus

'During the fray [May 12, between part of Grant's army and a Confederate detachment], a [soldier] staggered and fell to earth; at the same time a piercing cry was heard in the house near by. Examination of the wounded soldier showed that a bullet had passed through the scrotum and carried away the left testicle. The same bullet had apparently penetrated the left side of the abdomen of … [a] young lady mid-way between the umbilicus and the anterior spinous process of the ileum, and become lost in the abdomen. This daughter suffered an attack of peritonitis, but recovered. … Two hundred and seventy-eight days after the reception of the minié ball, she was delivered of a fine boy, weighing eight pounds, to the surprise of herself and the mortification of her parents and friends. … The doctor … concluded that … the same ball that had carried away the testicle of his young friend … had pene-

85

trated the ovary of the young lady, and, with some spermatazoa upon it, had impregnated her. With this conviction he approached the young man and told him the circumstances. The soldier appeared skeptical at first, but consented to visit the young mother; a friendship ensued which soon ripened into a happy marriage.'*

* The American Weekly, *November 4, 1874; quoted in Gould and Pyle,* Anomalies and Curiosities of Medicine. *Philadelphia: The Julien Press, 1896.*

Ill Wind

When a cow has an attack of bloat (actually methane gas generated in the stomach) it must obtain relief promptly or it is likely to die.

A Dutch veterinarian was summoned recently to treat a cow suffering from this affliction, an agricultural news service reported. He tried a standard remedy, which is to insert a tube carefully up the beast's rear end.

A satisfying rush of gas followed.

With misplaced scientific zeal, the vet, perhaps seeking a source of cheap heat and light, then applied a match.

The resulting torchlike jet set the barn ablaze. It burned to the ground. The flames spread to the near-by fields, which were consumed.

The vet was convicted of negligence and fined.

The cow remained serene.

A Difficult Patient

Henrik Ibsen spent the last six years of his life,

unable to write, staring out of his window in Christiania.

One day when a nurse announced that he was feeling better, the old curmudgeon found the ultimate putdown. 'On the contrary!' he said, and died. – *Time*, September 1971

Happy End

ATLANTA – Surgeons in Atlanta have successfully restored a severed penis to its owner, after it had been chopped off in a crime of passion. A 20-year-old man in rural South Carolina lost the organ to a butcher's knife wielded by his girl friend's estranged husband. Though it took six hours to get the victim to Atlanta's Emory University Hospital, the penis was put on ice and made the trip in satisfactory condition. Working for three hours, six Emory surgeons joined the organ's vein, two arteries and two nerves. When the victim went home a few weeks later, the penis was reportedly in full working order.* – *Moneysworth*

*The Washington Post *account added that the assailant had been indicted for 'mayhem'.*

Diagnosis

The last words of Joseph Henry Green, the great English surgeon, were (pointing to his heart), 'Congestion'; and then (taking his own pulse), 'Stopped.'

Wide-Eyed

Merle Oberon underwent so many facelifts that she had to sleep with her eyes open. – *Esquire* magazine, March 1983.

PEJORATIVES

Banal

A *ban* once meant a proclaimed order: Indo-European *bha*, 'speak'. Marriage *banns*, proclaiming a couple's engagement, are still posted on church doors in Catholic countries.

A French *banlieue* or 'ban-place', now 'suburb', referred to the area controlled by a local authority; where its 'writ ran', as lawyers say.

A *moulin à ban* or *four à ban* was a mill or an oven which the lord of the manor provided for his tenants to use in common in return for a share of the output.

The French, and then English, *banal* came from this idea of the common or usual.

Curmudgeon

The origin of this term is a mystery. An anonymous correspondent wrote to Dr. Samuel Johnson suggesting that the word came from *coeur méchant*, French for an 'evil heart'.

In his great dictionary, Johnson accepted this notion, suggesting that *curmudgeon* derived from '*coeur méchant*, Fr. [meaning *from*] an unknown correspondent'.

Then in 1775, *Ash's Dictionary*, in a demented theft from Johnson, announced that *curmudgeon* came 'from the French *coeur*, unknown, and *méchant*, a correspondent'.

curmudgeon

Dunce

The lifelong concern of the great medieval Franciscan theologian *Duns Scotus** was rebutting the theological ideas of the rival order of Dominicans, particularly those of Thomas Aquinas.

Although Duns Scotus succeeded well enough at

the time, in later centuries his followers, known as
Dunses, were counterattacked as dullards and
obscurantists.

And with *dunce* the Dominicans seem to have had
the last word.

* Properly, John Duns Scotus; *i.e.,* John *of* Duns *in Berwickshire,* Scotland.

Hip, Hip, Hurrah!

A Crusader war-cry. HEP is *Hierusalemma Est
Perdita,* 'Jerusalem is lost'; *huraj* is 'forward' in
Armenian.

Ostracize

The Greeks wrote names on fragments of broken
pottery or tile (*ostrakon,* literally, 'oystershell') as
ballots when voting to exile someone who represented a danger to the state.

Aristides the Just was once handed a potsherd by
an illiterate fellow citizen, who asked him to scratch
'Aristides' on it.

As Aristides started to write, he asked the man,
'What's so bad about Aristides?'

'I'm just tired of always hearing him called "the
Just",' the fellow replied.

Posh

The agreeable theory that this word designates the
preferred cabin arrangement on the P&O liners to
the Far East: 'Port Out, Starboard Home', to avoid the
afternoon sun in the Red Sea, cannot be proved. It

Posh

never occurs in the P&O's records. In the late 19th century it meant, simply, a dandy.

Sycophant

This word, whose modern sense is 'flattering parasite; informer', literally means 'fig-indicator': Greek *sukon*, 'fig', and *phantes*, 'one who shows'.

The original *sycophants* slyly uncovered dealers in smuggled or stolen figs – a substantial traffic at the time – and then denounced them to the police.

Tawdry

The convent, later cathedral, of Ely was founded in the 7th century by St. Audrey, who died of a growth in her throat, which she believed was a punishment for wearing sumptuous necklaces.

In time, a fair came to be held at Ely on St. Audrey's day, October 17, at which one of the most popular wares was 'St. Audrey's lace', a handsome chain or lace band for women to wear around their necks. *

As the centuries passed, the lace was made more and more shoddily, while the saint's name elided into *Tawdry*. †

* Lace, *which comes from Latin* laqueus, *'noose', via Old French* las, *originally meant 'neck-band'*.
† *Just as* St Clair *has collapsed into* Sinclair.

ADDITIONAL NAMES

LAKE TROUT*
Attorney
Los Angeles, California
Brother of Brook Trout.

LARRY DERRYBERRY*
Attorney General
Oklahoma City, Oklahoma
*Also Harry Derryberry, Lima, O., and Jerry Derryberry,
Chattanooga, Tenn.*

LAURA KNOTT TWINE
Weaver*
Norwich, Connecticut
The Compiler has a photograph of this establishment.

LAVENDER HANKEY*
Los Angeles, California
Compare Lacey Pantti, Republic, Mich.

LAVENDER SIDEBOTTOM *
Masseuse, Elizabeth Arden
New York City

* N.b.: Epitaph of Mr. Longbottom, who died young: Arse
longa, vita brevis.

LAWLESS & LYNCH
Attorneys
Jamaica, New York

LEE BUM SUCK *
Foreign Minister
Seoul, South Korea

** Captain Robert E. Lee, U.S.N. (Ret.), noise monitor for the
Montgomery County (Md.) Environmental Protection
Department, changed his name to Roberto Edouardo
Leon to qualify for 'affirmative action' promotions ahead
of his peers. 'Finding loopholes is my job,' he said.
'This is an insult to Hispanics,' fumed the governor's
Commissioner on Hispanic Affairs.*

LEGRUNT E. CRAPPER *
Johns Hopkins Hospital
Baltimore, Maryland

(Harvard Medical School *Alumni Bulletin*)

** His doctor reports that his name may subsequently have
been changed to LeGrant.*

95

LE NO FUCK BÉBÉ
French Rock Combo*

(Le Matin)

* The Compiler has a photograph of this grouping.

LESBIA LOBO*
Golfer

* Winner of the 1953 Broadmoor Ladies Invitational Golf Tournament in Colorado Springs, Colo.

LETTICE GOEDEBED
Johannesburg, South Africa

LINUS KLUEMPER*
Jasper, Indiana

* Attained celebrity in August 1955 when a fan in his bedroom window wriggled five feet towards him and chopped off the big toe of his right foot.

LOBELIA RUGTWIT HILDEBIDDLE
Psychology Student
Occidental College
Los Angeles, California

LOCH NESS HONTAS
Tulane University Medical School
New Orleans, Louisiana

LO FAT*
Retired Merchant Seaman
New York City

* Compare Shark Ho, New York City.

LOUIS GEORGE MAURICE ADOLPH ROCH
ALBERT ABEL ANTONIO ALEXANDRE NOÉ JEAN
LUCIEN DANIEL EUGÈNE JOSEPH-LE-BRUN
JOSEPHE-BARÊME THOMAS THOMAS THOMAS
THOMAS PIERRE ARBON PIERRE-MAUREL
BARTHELEMI ARTUS ALPHONSE BERTRANI
DIEUDONNÉ EMANUEL JOSUÉ VINCENT LUC
MICHEL JULES-DE-LA-PLANE JULES-BAZIN JULIO

CESAR JULLIEN *
Orchestra Conductor
Sisteron, France

Born in 1812 and named for members of his father's orchestra, the Maestro was for obvious reasons known simply as The Conductor Jullien. On 15 June 1854, he presented 'The Fireman's Quadrille' in the Crystal Palace in New York. At the climax, by prearrangement, flames burst out, engine bells rang in the streets, the windows were broken and firemen burst in, spewing water from their hoses. Dozens of spectators collapsed as the crowd fought to leave the hall. Jullien died, insane, in 1856.

LOVEY NOOKEY GOOD *
Texas State Health Department
Austin, Texas

Compare Cassandra Nookiesnatch (possibly of Eskimo origin).

LOYAL LODGE NO. 296 KNIGHTS OF PYTHIAS PONCA CITY OKLAHOMA SMITH *
Ponca City, Oklahoma

Born August, 21, 1876. Mencken, op. cit.

97

LUSCIOUS PEA
The Charity Hospital
New Orleans, Louisiana

LYNDA WHYNOT*
Wanton
Providence, Rhode Island

*Convicted of lewd and wanton behaviour in the Gemini
Hotel* (Providence Journal).

LYULPH YDWALLO ODIN NESTOR EGBERT
LYONEL TOEDMAG HUGH ERCHENWYNE SAXON
ESA CROMWELL ORMA NEVILL DYSART
PLANTAGENET TOLLEMACHE-TOLLEMACHE
Bentleigh, Otumoetai,
Tauranga, New Zealand

(Burke's Peerage and Baronetage)

SPORT

Hare Trigger

Near Louisville, Kentucky, a rabbit reached out of a hunter's game bag, pulled the trigger of his gun, and shot him in the foot. – *The New Yorker*, May 1947

Hunting Season Opens

ROME – Italy's hunting season began yesterday – with the hunters falling almost as fast as the pheasants.

The 'bag' totalled at least nine people wounded and thousands more hurt in fighting over who had shot what.

The victims include two men who dropped dead in the excitement of the chase.

A hunter who fled is wanted for manslaughter and 'failure to succour' a man he killed by mistake.

Another hunter was accidentally shot dead as he and a man argued over who had brought down a pheasant.

In the countryside outside Turin a grief-stricken hunter turned his shotgun on himself after accidentally killing a man walking behind him, but two others overpowered him before he could pull the trigger.

Many of the stalking hunters were shot because they wore Alpine hats with plumes in them. The plumes were mistaken for pheasants. – London *Sun*

Mixed Bag

Lord Tennyson, in the 1850s, invited a Russian nobleman to his house on the Isle of Wight and used to send him off with a gun in the mornings to walk the hedgerows. One day the Russian came back looking pleased with himself and reported in a thick Slav accent that he had shot two peasants. Tennyson

mixed bag

corrected him, saying 'two pheasants'. 'No,' said the Count, 'two peasants. They were insolent, so I shot them.' *

*Jonathan Garnier Ruffer, The Big Shots – Edwardian Shooting Parties. London: Debrett's Peerage Ltd., 1977.

Royal Sport

The King of France and a party of 13 during an 18-day hunt in 1775, employing spears and hawks as well as guns, killed 47,950 head of game.

Sporting Print

Lord Charles Beresford* had an entire fox hunt – the Waterford hounds – tattooed in full cry on his back: hounds, horses, and riders, all in gorgeous colour.

The fox, in this tableau, was just going to earth in the nearest hole, down which its brush was shown disappearing.

* 'Charlie B.' once telegraphed to decline an invitation: 'So sorry can't come. Lie follows by post.'
Cf. Geoffrey Bennett, Charlie B. London: Peter Dawnay Ltd. 1968.

Dead Ducks

Dr. Ernest J. Fox, a veterinarian, of Georgetown, South Carolina, and his friend, Marshall Trueluck, went duck shooting at Annandale Plantation in 1976.

Two single birds, coming from opposite directions, whistled in to look at the decoys.

They cracked head on with great force. Both splashed into the water, stone dead.

Out of the Frying Pan

BY OUR SAO PAULO CORRESPONDENT – A man who went fishing on the banks of the Amazon's Rio Negro was attacked by infuriated bees after he struck their nest while trying to free his line from a tree.

To escape, he leapt into the river – and was devoured by piranhas. – London *Daily Telegraph*

HIGH FINANCE

Bearish

An ancient proverb in many languages warns against selling a bear skin before you have caught the bear. Thus, for centuries, in English financial jargon stock sold 'short' – that is, stock one did not own but sold anyway, hoping to repurchase it cheaper – was known as a 'bear skin'. The seller was described as a 'bear-skin jobber', or 'bear': one who stands to profit from a decline in the quotation for a stock; a pessimist.

His opponent, the optimist, has been designated a 'bull' at least since the early 18th century.

Capital

From Latin *caput*, a 'head' of cattle. Cattle are one of the oldest forms of wealth: they are movable, grow, bear interest (milk), and provide capital gains (calves). Homer valued Ajax's shield in ox hides, and in many cultures a bride-price or damages at law are set in cattle.

Not surprisingly, a number of our financial words derive from this source. *Pecuniary* and *peculation* come from Latin *pecus*, 'herd', and *chattel* is cognate with *cattle*.

The Wall Street expression *watered stock* describes cattle who, given salt shortly before reaching a convenient stream, imbibe grossly, increase their weight, and thus fetch an inflated price.

Company

The original sense of *company* survives in our expression, 'We're having *company* for dinner'; that is, persons with whom one 'breaks bread': Latin *com*, 'together', and *panis*, 'bread'.

The business title *& Co.* adds to *company* an ampersand: &, which is the last surviving symbol from the oldest known system of shorthand, invented by Marcus Tiro about 63 B.C., and for centuries used in the Roman courts, to abbreviate *et*, 'and'. It is called *ampersand* because school recitations of letters once began 'A *per se* A' and ended '& *per se* And'.

Dicker

The Romans used to demand bundles of ten (*decuria*) furs or hides from conquered German tribes as tribute. Over time, the Germans transformed *decuria* into *decura* and later *decher*.

The word reached England and Holland in the Middle Ages as *dyker*. The colonists brought it to America as *dicker* and used it when bartering for furs with the Indians.

From that meaning it evolved into its present sense of 'haggle'.

Garnish

In business terminology you *garnish* or *garnishee* the salary of someone who owes you money by making his employer turn over part of it to you until the debt is extinguished.

In cooking, to garnish means to 'embellish', as by adding a sprig of parsley.

The two words come from the same source, Old French *garnir*, to 'prepare', 'embellish', or 'warn'. A fortified town was once called *garnished*, or 'prepared'. When a warning was issued about the creditworthiness of a person encumbered by debt, he was also said to be *garnished*.

Money

The Romans of the 3rd century B.C., like other people of antiquity, attached their mint to a temple, that of Juno *Moneta*, the 'admonisher', from *monere*, 'warn'. In time, the coins and the mint itself also became known as *moneta*, which is still the Italian word. This gave Spanish *moneda* and French *monnaie*, which then gave English *money*, and Old English *mynet*, 'coins', whence English *mint*. *Moidore* comes from Portuguese *moeda de ouro*, 'coin of gold'.

Dollar comes from *Joachimsthal*, 'Joachim's valley' (*thal*) in Bohemia, where in the early 16th century the first *thaler* was minted.

The Spanish dollar, or piece of eight, was the most widely circulated coin in America before the revolution. The $ sign may be a modified figure 8, to signify that coin, or the initials *U* and *S* superimposed; or a modified £ sign; or, quite possibly, a Phoenician symbol for strength and sovereignty. (There were extensive exchanges between the Phoenicians and the ancient Iberians.) The Spanish believe that the $ sign represents the pillars of Hercules on either side of the Strait of Gibraltar, bound together under Spanish rule.

Philately

This comparatively recent word for the study of postage stamps means literally in Greek, 'love of not being taxed', since a stamp meant the letter was carried without further payment.

Similarly, the Modern Greek word for 'post office' is *tachydromeion*, 'quick-running place' (cf. *Postman*).*

*I particularly like the Modern Greek expression for 'national bank': literally, it is an 'ethnic trapeze', ethniki trapeza. And to pay the bill in a restaurant is to 'canonize the logarithm', while a 'love affair' is an 'erotic hypothesis'. A military officer in civvies is said to be wearing 'political clothes', from polis, 'city'.

Salary

Salt is indispensable to human life. Foraging animals concentrate salt in their bodies; when we lived as hunters, we got our salt from their flesh. But after we settled down to row-crop agriculture we had to get it artificially, through mining it or boiling or evaporating seawater.

As human settlement spread out from places where salt could be made, more and more it became an object of commerce. All the early caravan tracks across the desert were salt routes, as was the oldest road in Europe, Italy's *Via Salaria*.

The *salarium* was an allowance given to Roman soldiers to buy salt. The word reached us as *salary*.

Tally

Instead of issuing written receipts in financial transactions, from Norman times on the Royal Exchequer cut notches into 'tally sticks' (from Latin *talea*, 'stick') to indicate amounts of money involved.

The stick, usually about a foot long, but sometimes over six feet, was then split in two. The Exchequer retained one half and gave the other to the second party in the deal. The officials who kept the sticks were called *telliers*, now *tellers*.

In 1834 the authorities resolved to get rid of this hopelessly cumbersome system. The centuries' accumulation of sticks was burned in the furnace of the House of Lords.

The excessive charge of fuel set the building afire. Both Houses of Parliament burned to the ground.

EXTRA NAMES

MACGREGOR SUZUKI
Montreal, Canada

MADONNA GHOSTLY
Teacher
Washington, D.C.

MAGDALENA BABBLEJACK
(*Maclean's* magazine)

MRS. MAGINIS OYSTER
Social Leader
San Rafael, California
(Social Register)

MAJOR MINOR
U.S. Army

MAJOR QUAINTANCE
U.S. Army
(The New Yorker)

MANLESS LAWRENCE*
Virginia
(Division of Vital Records and Health Statistics,

Department of Health, Richmond, Virginia)
*Illegitimate. Compare Wedless Souvenir Campbell
(Florida Bureau of Vital Statistics).*

MARK CLARK VAN ARK
Toledo, Ohio

MARMALADE P. VESTIBULE
Door-to-door Firewood Salesman
Cambridge, Massachusetts

MARY LOUISE PANTZAROFF*
Huron County, Ohio
Compare Mary Maloof Teabaggy, Boston, Mass.

MAUSOLEUM JACKSON
Virginia
(Division of Vital Records and Health Statistics,
Department of Health, Richmond, Va.)

MELISSY DALCINY CALDONY YANKEE PANKEE DEVIL-TAKE-THE-IRISHMAN GARRISON
Tryon City, North Carolina

MEMBRANE PICKLE
Virginia
(Division of Vital Records and Health Statistics,
Department of Health, Richmond, Va.)

(MISS) MEMORY LANE
Roslyn High School, New York

Mary Maloof Teabaggy, Boston

MEMORY LEAKE
Contractor
Tupelo, Mississippi

MENE MENE TEKEL UPHARSIN POND
Hartford, Connecticut

MERCY BUMPUS *
Wife of 'General Tom Thumb'

** Enjoyed the specialised distinction of being fought over
by the General and his tiny rival, Commodore Nutt.*

(MISS) MIGNON HAMBURGER
University of Wisconsin
Madison, Wisconisn

MING-TOY EPSTEIN *
New York City

** Long questioned by the Compiler, Ming-Toy's
authenticity has been established by S. J. Perelman and
others.*

MINNIE MAGAZINE
Editor, *Time* magazine
New York City

MOO, BOO, GOO, and LITTLE MISS MAY
New Orleans, Louisiana

MOON UNIT ZAPPA and DWEEZLE ZAPPA
Hollywood, California

MUFFY VIRGIN
Student
University of Chattanooga, Tennessee

111

Minnie Magazine, Magazine Editor

MUSTAFA KUNT*
Turkish Military Attaché
Moscow, U.S.S.R.

* Occasion of much ribald official cable traffic, along with his vis-à-vis, Major R. Rectanus, U.S. Assistant Military Attaché, Moscow. Of Gen. Plastiras (Greece) Winston Churchill expressed the hope that he did not have 'feet of clay'.

112

LAW AND DISORDER

Crossfire

Two gangsters, James Gallo and Joe Conigliaro, set about to murder a stool pigeon, Vinny Ensulo, alias Vinnie Ba Ba, alias Vincent Ennisie.

On November 1, 1973, they jumped him on Columbia Street, Brooklyn, and took him for a ride. Gallo pointed a gun at his head from the right, and Conigliaro covered him from the left. The car swerved violently. The two gangsters shot each other.*

*The New York Daily News described the sequel. 'Conigliaro, hit in the spine, was paralyzed. Every year after that Vinny Ensulo sent wheelchair batteries to Conigliaro. A small card with the batteries always said, "Keep rolling, from your best pal, Vinny Ba Ba." '

Ms. Cooperman's Discomfiture

A woman named Cooperman recently went to court in New York to change her name to 'Cooperperson'.

Judge Scileppi denied the petition, on the grounds of 'inanity'.

Grit

During a motel holdup in Cleveland on May 3, 1977, the robber, Bruce Williams, was shot and paralyzed from the waist down.

He impressed the authorities the following year by committing five additional crimes within three months, including a robbery, a theft, and a kidnapping. The Associated Press in May 1978 quoted his comment on the work of the Cleveland police: 'They pick on me,' he said, from his wheelchair.

Cover-up

Of Pope John's trial at the Council of Constance in 1414–1418, Gibbon records that 'The most scandalous charges were suppressed; the vicar of Christ was only accused of piracy, rape, murder, sodomy and incest.'*

This council was also attended by seven hundred harlots, according to reliable authorities – fifteen hundred, according to others.

Wheeler-Peelers

GRAND RAPIDS, MICHIGAN – A local striptease joint must build ramps on its stage to accommodate handicapped strippers, state officials have ruled. – *Reuter*

Copulation

Charlotte Oxford Tyler, mother of one, admitted during an investigation in Memphis in December 1973 to having had sex with several hundred policemen.*

Under questioning, she stated that this 'may have had something to do with my belief in law and order'.

Together with 500 in the mid-South area, according to some press accounts. Asked about the inconveniences of sex in squad cars with officers wearing guns, truncheons, bullet belts, handcuffs, and angular badges, she replied, according to the Press-Scimitar, *'It's just something you have to get used to working around.'*

Copulation

Evidence

PHILADELPHIA – A former Philadelphia fireman, in Federal Court here trying to overturn his dismissal for long hair, set his head on fire.

'It must have been the hairspray I used,' said the sheepish ex-fire-fighter, William Michini, who apparently tried to dramatize that his locks were not a safety threat to his job.

'Hair is self-extinguishing. It doesn't burn,' he boasted.

With that he struck a match and held it to his head, which caught fire. – *Associated Press*

EQUIPMENT

Ammonia

Ammonia is so called because it was first made from the dung of the worshippers' camels at the temple of Jupiter *Ammon* in Egypt.

Bonfire

A 'bone-fire', in which the bodies of the slain were burned after a battle, or a heretic was burned at the stake, or corpses cremated.

Loo

Nobody (except the estimable Thomas Crapper, who perfected the flush toilet) seems eager to accept responsibility for what goes on in the W.C. Both the French and English words for these matters imply that it all started somewhere else.

Thus, *loo* is considered in England to be a 'Frenchy' genteelism, like *demi-tasse*. However, the actual French expression is *lieu à l'Anglaise*, 'English place', which throws it right back across The Channel (or alternatively it may come from Anglo-French '*gardez l'eau*', shouted when throwing slops into the street from a window).

And one of the most common French words for toilet is *le water*, from the English 'water closet'.

But the English *toilet* is again a French word,

toilette, meaning a 'little cloth' spread on a lady's bedside table, where the things she might need overnight would be laid out.

Loo

Lumber

The Lombards (*Langobardi* in Latin, or 'long-beards') were a Germanic tribe who in the 6th century implanted themselves in the Po Valley. Although they were detested there, the area became known as *Lombardy*. Their kingdom was overthrown by the Franks under Charlemagne. Centuries later a number of Lombards spread around Europe as traders and moneylenders. They brought with them the three-ball sign of the pawnbroker, presumably adapted from the arms of the Medici.

London's Lombard Street contained numerous money-lending establishments, essentially pawn-shops, which were called *lombards*, pronounced 'lumbers'.

The rooms where pawned property was stored thus became *lumber* rooms. That term later came to cover store-houses in general, and finally what they sometimes contain: sawn timber.

Pocket-handkerchief

A *poke* (from French *poche*) is a sack, as in the 'pig in a poke' that one should think twice about buying. A small *poke* is a *pocket*.

Chef in French is 'head' (from Latin *caput*), and a *couvre-chef*, or *kerchief*, is a head-cloth or bandanna. One you keep in hand to sneeze into is a *hand couvre-chef* or *handkerchief*.

So *pocket-handkerchief* means 'little-sack-hand-cover-head'.

Sarcophagus

Literally, 'flesh-eater'. The Greeks had a direct way of looking at things.

On the other hand, their word for 'cemetery', *koimeterion*, means 'sleeping place'.

Wig

Wig comes from *periwig*, from the French *perruque*, 'wig', which comes from *perroquet*, 'parrot', a reference to decorative plumage, just as the English called a dandy a 'popinjay'.

Perroquet, however, is derived from *Pierrot*, a diminutive of *Pierre*, 'Peter'.* (*Parrot* is also a Peter diminutive.)

That saint, whose attempt to walk on water is described in Matthew 14:29, also gave his name to another bird, the stormy *petrel*, which can live on the waves far out to sea.

Sailors call petrels 'Mother Carey's chickens', perhaps by folk-etymology, via a Latin language, from *mater cara*, the 'dear mother' Mary.

Personal names frequently become attached to birds (and animals), e.g., jackdaw, robin redbreast (originally just redbreast), magpie, tomtit, dickey bird, jack rabbit.

EVEN MORE NAMES

Napoleon B. Barefoot*
Judge
Wayne Co. Superior Court
Goldsboro, N.C.

*Compare Judge Barefoot Sanders, U.S. District Court,
Dallas, Tex.*

Needa Climax
Methodist Church Officer
Centerville, Louisiana

Never Fail*
Louisville, Kentucky

*Mrs. Never Fail, exasperated by her husband's accounts of
his achievements with 'beautiful blondes', finally sought
divorce* (United Press). *Compare Never Fail, Jr., builder,
Tulsa, Okla. (known to the Compiler).*

Newton Hooton
Cambridge, Massachusetts

N. Guppy*
The Pond, Haddenham,
Cambridgeshire, England

*Known to the Compiler. The fish is named for the family,
not vice versa. In 1978 Barrister Michael Fysh defended a
fishing rights case in the House of Lords before Lord
Salmon.*

NITA BATH
(Philadelphia Evening Bulletin)

NOBLE PUFFER
Superintendent of Schools
Cook County, Illinois

NOBLE TEAT*
Still Pond, Maryland

* Compare Faithful Teate, Dublin 'who wrote a quaint poem on the Trinity' (Encyclopedia Britannica). *Also Noble Buffer, Superintendent of Schools, Cook Co., Illinois; Noble Tickle, Rating, Royal Navy; Noble Butt, Boston; Noble Dick, Chairman, Dick Corporation, Pittsburgh, Pa.*

NOEL T. TWEET
(Business Week)

NOSMO KING*
Pikesville, Maryland

* Named for sign in waiting room of Dr. Brull, Sugarcane Road, Pikesville.

NOVICE FAWCETT
President, Ohio State University
Columbus, Ohio

NOWAY NEAR WHITE *
Shoe Salesman
Columbus, Ohio
*Compare January Snow White, Tampa, Fla.

ODILE, ODELIA, OLIVE, OLIVER, OLIVIA,
OPHELIA, ODELIN, OCTAVE, OCTAVIA, OVIDE,
ONESIA, OLITE, OTTO, ORMES, and OPTA
MAYNARD *
Abbeville, Louisiana

*Dunkling, op. cit. Compare Assumpta, Attracta,
Concepta, Redempta and Rejoyca Custigan, of
Ballybunion, Ireland, who won a traditional dance
competition 'because of their intricate footwork and they
did not kick too high'.

ODIOUS CHAMPAGNE *
Paper Mill Employee
Winslow, Maine
*Compare Romeo Q. Champagne, state official, N.H.

O. HELL *
Contractor
Alto Adige, Italy
*Known to the Compiler.

SIR OLATERU OBA ALAIYELUWA OLEGBEGI II,
the Olowo of Owo *

* 'Son of Oba Alaiyeluwa Olabegi I; married, many sons
and daughters; Educated, Owo Government School;
Treasury Clerk in Owo Native Administration;
Address, P.O. Box 1, Afin Oba Olowo, Owo;
Telephone number: Owo 1' (Who's Who).

124

OLDMOUSE WALTZ
Federal Writers Project
New Orleans, Louisiana

OOFTY GOOFTY BOWMAN *
Shakespearean Actor
Racine, Wisconsin
(Milwaukee *Sentinel*)

* Named after a Ringling Bros. clown.

OPHELIA TITTEY *
Fall River, Massachusetts

* Compare Ophelia Bumps (reported by hospital where she was a patient), Ophelia Legg, Norwalk, Ohio, and Ophelia Butts, Chattanooga, Tenn.

FATHER O'PRAY *
Church of St. Ignatius Loyola
New York City

* Compare Rev. Goodness, Church of the Ascension, New York City, Rev. Hosanna, Denver, Colo., and Rev. God of Congaree, S.C.

ORAL BLOW *
Portsmouth, Virginia
(Bureau of Vital Statistics, State Board of Health, Richmond, Virginia)

* Birth certificate examined by the Compiler. Compare fellow-Virginian Easy Blow (who changed her name to Esther) and Oral Love, nursing home proprietor, Portland, Oregon.

ORANGE MARMALADE LEMON
Wichita, Kansas

ORIGINAL BUG *
Liverpool, England
(Liverpool Echo)

** Compare Septimus Bugg (London News Chronicle).
A Mr. Bugbee put himself on the entomological map by
donating 30,000 parasitic wasps to the Smithsonian
Institution* (Washington Post).

Original Bug, Liverpool

OSCAR ASPARAGUS *
Basketball Star

(*Maclean's* magazine)

* Compare Baskerville Holmes, basketball player, Memphis State University, Memphis, Tenn.

Oscar Asparagus, Basketball Star

OSBORN OUTHOUSE *
Boston, Massachusetts

* Compare A. Purdey Outhouse, perennial upper New York State office-seeker.

GETTING THERE
IS HALF THE FUN

Predestination

The Bishop of Exeter, William Cecil (1863–1936), travelling by rail to perform a confirmation ceremony, misplaced his ticket and was unable to produce it when requested by the conductor.

'It's quite all right, my Lord,' said the conductor reassuringly, 'we know who you are.'

'That's all very well,' answered the bishop, 'but without the ticket how am I to know where I'm going?' *

* *Lord David Cecil mentions that the fifth Marquess of Salisbury (intermittently Prime Minister, 1885–1902) 'found it hard to recognize his fellow men, even his relations, if he met them in unexpected circumstances. Once, standing behind the throne at a Court ceremony, he noticed a young man smiling at him. "Who is my young friend?" he whispered to a neighbour. "Your eldest son," the neighbour replied.'*

Rescue

VERO BEACH, FLORIDA – Firemen were having enough trouble trying to wrestle an 1,800-pound horse out of a septic tank. The concrete roof of the tank gave way when the horse walked across the soil covering it, and the beast wound up mired to its shoulders in what septic tanks are designed to hold.

After a few false starts, the firemen were able to pull the horse to safety with an auto tow truck. They thought their smelly job was over.

That was just before a skunk wandered onto the scene, raised his tail, and gave everybody present a couple of shots for good measure. It's not known whether he had a rough day in the woods or he just didn't like the stink the horse incident caused.* – Philadelphia *Bulletin*

In a similar episode, Larry Cavner, who runs a highway tow-truck operation in San Diego, was called by a motorist who was stuck in the mud of San Diego Bay. He went to the rescue in his tow truck. The tow truck got stuck. He summoned a backup tow truck to rescue the first one. It got stuck too. He then hired (or chartered) a huge amphibious vehicle, which started hauling out the backup tow truck. Alas, the huge amphibious vehicle itself got stuck. Desperate, Mr. Cavner then hired a bulldozer to rescue the other four vehicles. The bulldozer finally succeeded. Cavner estimated that the whole operation cost him $16,000. The original motorist waltzed away without paying.

That's Baseball

The Empress Eugénie staggered from the gory debris of her carriage after a bomb attack in which ten persons were killed and about 140 wounded.

'*C'est le métier*,'* she pronounced philosophically.

* '*It's all in the day's work.*'
  The attempted assassination of Napoleon III and the Empress was carried out on January 14, 1858, outside the Opéra.
  Cf. Harold Kurtz: The Empress Eugénie, 1826–1920. Boston: Houghton Mifflin, 1964.

Traffic

In 1895 there were only two cars in the whole state of Ohio. They collided.

The Glory that Was Greece

L'Abbé Fourmont's innovation in classical travel was

to obliterate the wonders of antiquity after he had inspected them.

'For the last month,' he wrote in 1729, 'thirty and sometimes forty or sixty workers have been smashing, destroying, *exterminating* the town of Sparta.

'This was the only way to make my trip a real hit

That's baseball

(*rendre illustre mon voyage*). Imagine my joy if you can . . . Sparta is the fifth city of the Morea that I have torn down . . . I did not reprieve Argos or Phylasia.'

GAMES

Canter

After the martyrdom and sanctification of Thomas à Becket under Henry II, the saint's grave in Canterbury cathedral became a place of pilgrimage – whence Chaucer's *Canterbury Tales*, told by a group of pilgrims on their way to the shrine.

The gait of their horses became known as the *canterbury*, later the *canter*.

Chess

The object of chess is to trap the *shah*, 'king'. The winner then announces that the king is 'dead' (*mat*): 'check-mate', or *shah* mat*.

Shah evolved, through an Old French plural, *esches*, into *chess*; also into *checkers*, both the game and the design.

The *Exchequer*, which in England deals with the financial side of government, probably derived from the checkerboard tables, *eschequier*, used in the Middle Ages to facilitate counting. A bank *check* comes from the same source.

The game of chess seems to have entered Europe with the Arabs, at the time of their conquest of Spain. They had learned it from the Persians, who apparently found it in India.

---

* *Perhaps also* sheikh.

Hazard

The *hazards* of life once referred to dice. The word comes from Arabic *az-zahr*, 'the die'. The Crusaders probably brought it back with them to France, whence, as *les hasards*, it crossed to England with the Normans. Some variants of craps are thus called the *hazards game*.

Ouija

The *ouija* board comes from French *oui* (yes) and German *ja* (yes).

Tennis

Tennis is sometimes said to come from French *tenez*, 'hold', a cry supposedly uttered by French players of this ancient Arabic game. But there is no record of such a cry, and the earliest occurrence of even the conjecture is in the 17th century; while *tenetz*, the English adaptation of the original Arabic word, *tanaz*, 'leap', goes back to 1400.

Racquet probably comes from Arabic *rahet*, 'palm of the hand'. The original form of the game was played with the palm alone.

The *c* in racquet doesn't belong there, being a garbling of French *raquette* and English *racket*.

The King of Diamonds

Memorializes Julius Caesar.

YOU NAME IT!

PAFIA PIFIA PEFIA POFIA PUFIA DA COSTA
Brazil
(Financial Times)

DR. PARADISE GARDEN *
Ear Surgeon
Toronto, Ontario
* *Changed his name to Dr. Eden.*

PEARL HARBOR
Telephone Operator of the *Birmingham News*
Birmingham, Alabama

PEARLIE RASH
Toledo, Ohio
(Toledo *Blade*)

PENINNAH SWINGLE HOGENCAMP UMBACH
Spiritualist Minister
Charleston, South Carolina

DR. PENIS *
Plastic Surgeon
San Francisco, California
* *In a syndicated October 1980* New York Times *article
Dr. Penis advises women to have their breasts removed*

before signs of cancer appear. 'We can't afford to wait for cancers to be detected, because by that time they're likely to have spread,' he states.

MISS PENSIVE COCKE*
Secretary
U.S. Army Air Corps

* Compare Mrs. Seeman Glasscock; J. Badcock, Editor, London; B. Grocock, Teacher, Washington, D.C.; and D. Grewcock, Stockbroker, N.Y. The Koch Erecting Company is a major supplier to New York City. Cinderella Hardcock studied with the Art Instruction School, Minneapolis. Respectful attention is bestowed on the good Cornish family of Trebilcock and concerned awareness on Prof. A. O. J. Cockshut. Mrs. Peedee Cox is a Planned Parenthood counsellor in Corpus Christi, Tex. W. J. Uglow Woolcock appears in Boyle's Court Guide *for 1915. Cf. P. H. Reaney,* The Origin of English Surnames. London: Routledge and Kegan Paul, 1967, p. 209 et seq.*

PETER BETER*
Attorney
Washington, D.C.

* Pronounced beeter. Perennial unsuccessful candidate for governor of West Virginia. Compare Peter Orifice, Holliston, Mass.

PHILI B. DEBOO*
Professor of Geology
Memphis, Tennessee

* Compare Philander Philpott Pettibone (Maclean's Magazine).

PHILOMENA CUNEGUNDE WEWE *
Hawaii

Compare Steven Weewee, Indiana University student.

(MISS) PINK GASH *
Hendersonville, North Carolina

(The Saturday Review)

*Compare Miss Pinkey Dickey Dukes, Branchville,
South Carolina.*

PIROUETTE SPIEGEL
White House Staff*
Washington, D.C.

During Kennedy Administration.

PLATO FOUFAS
Real Estate
Chicago, Illinois

PLUMMER & LEEK
Plumbers
Sheringham, Norfolk

(The Times)

POSITIVE WASSERMANN JOHNSON *
Evanston, Illinois

* *'Probably represents the indelicate humor of a medical
student'. – H. L. Mencken,* The American Language, *Fourth
Edition, New York: Alfred A. Knopf, 1936.*

PRESERVED FISH, JR.*
New Bedford, Massachusetts

* Born in 1766; partner in firm said to market whale oil in two grades: 'good and bad'. His father and other forebears bore the same name. 'There is no foundation to the oft repeated story that his name was bestowed by a New Bedford fisherman who found him as an infant adrift at sea in an open boat' (Dictionary of American Biography).

Preserved Fish, Jr.

PRIMROSE GOO*
Hawaii

Compare Goo Gee Lo, Sidney, Australia, father of Fook Hing, Fook Sing, Fook Ling and Fook You (Sidney Morning Herald).

(MISS) PTARMIGAN TEALE*
Boston, Massachusetts

Daughter of E. W. Teale, naturalist. Compare (Mrs.) Birdie Peacock, Goldsboro, N.C.

QUO VADIS HARRIS
Medical Research Assistant
Cambridge, Massachusetts

(New England Journal of Medicine)

RADICAL LOVE*
Selective Service Registrant
Washington, D.C.

Compare Love Newlove, Toronto, Ont. Natania Schitlove changed her name to Laura Schitlove.

RAPER YOWLER
Dayton, Ohio

RAPID INTEGRATION
(Newsweek)

ROMAN PRETZEL*
Tel Aviv, Israel

A frequent correspondent in the Jerusalem Post.

RONALD SUPENA
Lawyer
(Philadelphia Evening Bulletin)

ROOSEVELT CABBAGESTALK*
Pittsburgh, Pennsylvania

(Philadelphia Inquirer, quoting *Advertising Age)*
* *Compare Zeditha Cabbagestalk, Safeway cashier,
Washington, D.C.*

ROSEBUD ROSENBLOOM
Ethical Culture School
New York City

ROSETTA STONE
New York City

ROSEY and DEWEY BUTT*
Sister and Brother
Peru, Indiana

* *Compare Rose Rump, Bettendorf, Iowa, and Rosie
Rump, San Francisco, Calif.; also Barbara Fatt Heine,
New York City* (New York Times).

ROSEY VICE*
Multiple Larcenist
Great Glemham
Suffok, England

* *Possessed of a notable 'green thumb', she was released
from confinement each spring to assist in planting.*

ROSY YASS *
Cincinnati, Ohio

* So taken with her maiden name that after marriage she maintained a separate telephone directory listing for it. Compare Rosey and Dewey Butt, sister and brother, Peru, Indiana; Rosie Rump, Bettendorf, Iowa; and Rosie Rump, San Francisco, Ca.

ARTS AND SCIENCES

The Zambian Space Programme

Quite early in the space race Minister of Space Nkoloso of Zambia announced that his country would have a man on the moon by 1970.

After a while reporters were invited to witness one of the programme's high points. An unfortunate individual was stuffed in a barrel, to which was fastened a rope looped around a stout tree. Strong assistants then whirled the barrel around and around the tree. It was explained that this experience would familiarize the man in the barrel with some of the problems of orbital flight.*

In another phase of the programme the future astronauts were rolled downhill in oil drums and trained to walk on their hands, said by the minister to be 'the only way humans can walk on the moon'.

1729

G. H. Hardy, the Cambridge mathematician, liked to describe his visit to Putney to call on the Indian mathematical prodigy Srinivasa Ramanujan, who was ill.

Hardy came in a cab with the number 1729. It was, he suggested, a dull number.

Ramanujan was indignant. 'It is a very interesting number,' he retorted. 'It is expressible as the sum of two cubes in two different ways.'*

They are $12^3 + 1^3$ and $10^3 + 9^3$.

Cf. G. H. Hardy, Ramanujan. *Cambridge: Cambridge University Press, 1940.*

The Dean's Humour

Jonathan Swift (author of *Gulliver's Travels*, and a clergyman) published a work under the *nom de plume* of Isaac Bickerstaff, entitled *Predictions for the Year 1708*. In it he foretold that a prominent figure he disliked, called John Partridge, editor of an almanac, would 'infallibly die upon the 29th of March next'.

On March 30, Swift, under a different pseudonym, published a confirmation that Partridge had indeed died.

The desperate victim struggled to refute this canard, but the public, including his readers, remained convinced that he was dead, and the new 'Partridge' merely an impostor who hoped to take over the business.

As a result, his almanac had to suspend publication. Partridge never found out who had engineered the savage hoax.*

* *Cf. Irwin Ehrenpris,* Swift. *New York: Methuen & Company, 1967.*

The Odd Guest

On a trip to Paris, the geographer Von Humboldt, after whom the Humboldt Current is named, asked an alienist friend (as psychiatrists were then called) if it would be possible to have dinner with a lunatic. The alienist was glad to oblige.

At dinner, one guest, of reserved manner, dressed in black with a white cravat, remained silent. The other, strangely attired and with his hair in disarray, babbled continuously with his mouth full.

During the fruit course Baron von Humboldt,

discreetly indicating this curious figure, muttered to his host, 'I like your lunatic . . . he amuses me.'

'But it's the other one who's the lunatic!' whispered the alienist. 'The man you're pointing at is Monsieur Honoré de Balzac!'

The odd guest

BIRDS & BEASTS

Cab

That modest but determined beast, the goat, prances about our language in many disguises. *Capers* about, one might say. *Capra*, Latin 'goat', gives us *caper*, *caprice*, and *capricious*. The leaps of a kid, *cabri* in French, gave *cabriole*, a frisky jump.

In the 18th century *cabriole* meant a light two-wheeled carriage drawn by one horse, doubtless because of its jaunty motion. As *cabriolet*, the vehicle rolled to England, where it shrivelled to *cab*.*

* *The English specialize in these brusque contractions. Thus,* mobile vulgus *(fickle crowd) became* mob; sine nobilitate *(without nobility) became* snob; *association football became* soccer; *university,* varsity; *public house,* pub; *zoological garden,* zoo; *and so on.*

Caterpillar

Literally, 'hairy cat', from the Old French *chatepelose*.

Gossamer

This word is a contraction of 'goose-summer', meaning late October and November.

At that time, the harvest being done, the geese are let into the fields to fatten on the stubble; often on those brilliant days the 'gossamer' spider-webs are perceived hanging among the half-bare branches.

145

Caterpillar

Pedigree

Originally, Middle French *pie de grue*, 'crane's foot',
from a symbol used to indicate lines of descent on
genealogical charts.

Tuxedo

Tuxedo in a Delaware Indian dialect means 'round foot', a euphemism for 'wolf'.

At Tuxedo Park, New York, that in 1896 Griswald Lorillard cut the tails off his evening coat to create the short dinner jacket, which thus became known as the *tuxedo* ... in more than one sense, 'wolf's clothing'.

Tuxedo

Ukulele

'Jumping flea' in Hawaiian: *uku*, meaning 'flea', and *lele*, meaning 'jumping'. It was the local nickname for Major Purvis, a retired British officer who popularized the instrument, which had been brought to the islands by Portuguese labourers. Presumably *ukulele* refers to the fingers darting among the strings.

Sandwith Drinker

WHAT'S IN A NAME

DR. SAFETY FIRST *
Tulsa, Oklahoma
Another Safety First is in his nineties in Seal Beach, Cal.

SALOME CASANOVA *
Havana, Cuba and Madrid, Spain
Known to the Compiler.

SANDWITH DRINKER
Class of 71
University of Pennsylvania

SANTIAGO NUDELMAN
Publisher
Brazil

SARA STRUGGLES NICELY
Clearwater, Florida
(Cleveland Plain Dealer)

MRS. SCREECH *
Singing Teacher
Victoria, British Columbia
Wife of Dr. Screech, Dentist.

149

SERIOUS MISCONDUCT*
Welwyn, England
Compare General Error, Pueblo, Colo.

SHAKEY T. MUDBONE
Hudson, New York

SHANDA LEAR*
Battle Creek, Michigan
Of the Lear Jet Lears.

SHINE SOON SUN*
Geophysicist
Houston, Texas

*Compare Moon Bong Kang, Korean Ambassador to
Switzerland. Dong-Dong Kong is a piano student at the
Julliard School of Music, New York City.*

SHLOMO TURTLEDOVE
Tel Aviv, Israel

LT. GEN. HIS HIGHNESS SHRI SHRI SHRI
SHRI SHRI SHRI SHRI SHRI SHRI SHRI
SHRI SHRI SHRI SHRI SHRI SHRI SHRI
SHRI SHRI SHRI SHRI SHRI SHRI SHRI
SHRI SHRI SHRI SHRI SHRI SHRI SHRI
SHRI SHRI SHRI SHRI SHRI SHRI SHRI
SHRI SHRI SHRI SHRI SHRI SHRI SHRI
SHRI SHRI SHRI SHRI SHRI SHRI SHRI
SHRI SHRI SHRI SHRI SHRI SHRI SHRI
SHRI SHRI SHRI SHRI SHRI SHRI SHRI
SHRI SHRI SHRI SHRI SHRI SHRI SHRI
SHRI SHRI SHRI SHRI SHRI SHRI SHRI
SHRI SHRI SHRI SHRI SHRI SHRI SHRI
SHRI SHRI SHRI SHRI SHRI SHRI SHRI
SHRI SHRI SHRI SHRI SHRI SHRI SHRI
SHRI SHRI SHRI SHRI SHRI SHRI SHRI
MAHARAJADHIRAJ RAJ RAJESHWAR SHRI
MAHARJA-I-RAJGAN MARARAJA SIR YADVINDRA
SINGH MAHENDRA BAHADUR, YADU
VANSHAVATANS BHATTI KUL BHUSHAN
RAJPRAMUKH OF PATIALA *
India and London, England

* Born in 1913, the Maharaja of Patiala is also the leader
of the Sikh community, all of whose members bear the
surname Singh (meaning lion). The sequence in the first
part of the title is usually contracted to 'Shri 108'.

SIDDHARTHA GREENBLATT
(Harper's Magazine)

151

Lt. Gen. H.H. Shri Shri Shri (etc... 108 times)
Maharajadhiraj, the Maharega of Patiala

SILENCE BELLOWS*
Editor, *Christian Science Monitor*

*Vermont Connecticut Royster was editor of the other
reliable American paper, the* Wall Street Journal.

COMMANDER SINK, U.S.N.
Fort Washington, Maryland

Commander Sink, U.S.N.

SODAWATER BOTTLEWALLA*
Bombay, India

(New York Times)

*Walla is a Parsee suffix indicating occupation,
comparable to the 'er' in Baker.*

SOLOMON GEMORAH
Brooklyn, New York

DR. STARK STARING
Professor, University of Utrecht
Holland

(Sunday Telegraph)

STRANGEWAYS PIGG STRANGEWAYS
Cricket Star
London, England

SUBMIT CLAPP*
Easthampton, Massachusetts

* Distant kinswoman of the Compiler. Married Asahel Clark (1737–1822). Mother of Eliakim, Eleasar, Submit, Asakel, Bohan (died in infancy), Bohan (the second), Electa, Jerusha, Achsah, Lucas and Jared.

(MISS) SUE YU
Library Card Holder
Flushing, New York

SUPARPORN POOPATTANA
New York City

SUPPLY CLAPP THWING
Harvard College (Class of 1837)

MRS. TACKABERRY MCADOO
Social Leader
New York City
(Social Register)

TARANTULA TURNER
New Orleans, Louisiana

Tarantula Turner, Schoolgirl

TAURA LOURA GOLDFARB
New York City

TETLEY IRONSIDE TETLEY JONES
Chairman, Tetley Tea Company
London, England

T. GUEMPEL GLOMP
(Allentown, Pennsylvania *Morning Call*)

T. FUD PUCKER TUCKER
Bountiful, Utah

THEANDERBLAST MISCHGEDEIGLE SUMP*
Insurance Agent
Orillia, Ontario
* Insists on the inclusion of his middle name.

T. HEE
Restaurant Employee
New York City

THEODOLPHUS J. POONTANG
Oakland, California
(San Francisco Examiner)

Mrs. Theresa Picnick*
Nutritionist
Worchester, Massachusetts

*Compare Bacon Chow, nutritionist, Johns Hopkins School of Public Health, Baltimore, Md., and Lo Fat, cook aboard S.S. President Wilson.

Mrs T. Picnick, nutritionist

THOMAS CRAPPER*
Inventor of flush toilet
London, England
*His biography is aptly titled Flushed With Pride.

THUSNELDA NEUSBICKLE
Wellesley College
Wellesley, Massachusetts

MRS. TINY SPRINKLE*
New York City
*Compare A. Tiny Hurt, Portland, Oregon.

TOPPIE SMELLIE
T.V. Chicken Coating Mix Endorser

TRAILING ARBUTUS VINES*
Cumberland Mountains, Tennessee
*Mencken, op. cit.

BUSINESS

I. D.

NEW YORK – Sharon Mitchell, heroine of the X-rated *Captain Lust*, was having trouble cashing a cheque at a New York bank because she was not carrying a driver's licence or any other identification.

She *was* carrying a magazine in which she appeared in the nude. She handed over the magazine, hitched her sweater up to her chin, and arranged herself in the same pose.

They cashed her cheque.* – London *Sunday Telegraph* Magazine

Anna Mingo, 18, a chambermaid of Teignmouth, England, manifested a similar pragmatism when she fell into a manhole. Thanks to her outstanding proportions (42-24-38), she stuck fast in the opening. 'No doubt about it, my bust saved me,' she announced happily to the press after she had been successfully extracted.

A Deal's a Deal

In 1890 an indigent Swede sold the rights to his body after death to the Royal Swedish Institute of Anatomy. The seller became rich and twenty years later applied to buy back the contract. The institute turned him down. The seller went to court. The institute fought the suit and won.

The institute then applied to the court for compensation on the grounds that two teeth had been extracted from its property without its permission. The future cadaver was forced to pay damages.

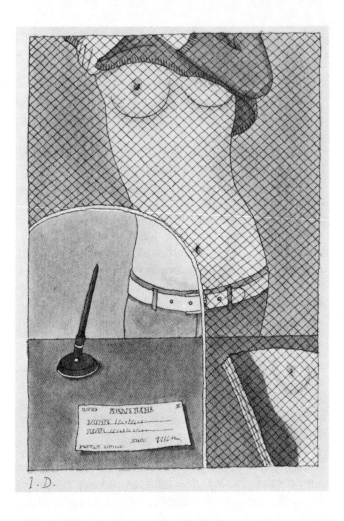

Investigate Before You Invest

The result of a door-to-door survey of five thousand typical Americans was reported by *Collier's* in May 1949. Asked what was bought and sold on the New York Stock Exchange, 64 percent replied, 'Livestock.'

Hot Seat

When the electric chair first became popular, shortly before the turn of the century, Emperor Menelik II of Ethiopia, hearing of this marvel, ordered it from America. Alas, it didn't work.

No one had told the emperor that for best results one needed electricity. Ethiopia had done.

The Abyssinian underworld relaxed. Menelik ordered the chair fitted up as a throne, which he put into regular service.

FOOD

Humble Pie

This sinister repast was composed of the *umbles*, or guts, of an animal, and was assigned to the servants, while the gentry enjoyed the steaks and chops.

Ketchup

In the 18th century the Dutch imported this Chinese condiment, originally a spiced mushroom sauce called *ketsiap*, as *ketjap*.

Luncheon

Lunch comes from Scottish *lonch*, a 'hunk' of meat.

Nuncheon, an old word for the midday meal, means 'noon drink' in Middle English: *nonechenche*.

So *luncheon*, a barbarous combination of the two, makes no sense, meaning, literally, 'drinking a hunk of meat'.

Marzipan

'Christ enthroned in judgement', *Christos Pantocrator*, was depicted on a Venetian coin. The Saracens were pleased to accept the cash, but not the theology, and so referred to these coins, which circulated widely, as *mauthaban*, 'seated king'.

Apparently the Venetians exacted the coin, which they came to call *matapanus*, as an import duty.*

Ketchup

In time it came to mean a percentage of a load of produce or merchandise, and eventually to a box that carried that percentage.

Still later it came to mean a similar box containing confections. By folk-etymology the word was then deformed into *Marci panis*, 'St Mark's bread'.

In the form of an almond paste candy, it came to

England as *marchpane*, the term used there until recently. It then reappeared via Germany as *marzi-pan*.

* Our dime, *similarly, comes from French* dîme, *a tax of a tenth of a load, from Latin* decem, *'ten'. Cf.* Dicker, *page 104.*

Mayonnaise

One of the few surviving words of Carthaginian derivation. Mago, Hannibal's brother, gave his name to Mahon, capital of Minorca. The Duc de Richelieu successfully beseiged it in 1756. During the seige his cook concocted the sauce from eggs and oil, there being no butter or cream on the island, and named it after the town.*

* Similarly, zabaglione *is said to be named after Marshal Baglioni, who defended Florence from Castruccio Castracani in the 15th century. Reduced to eggs and brandy, his cook invented 'Baglioni soup',* zuppa Baglioni *elided into* zabaglione.

Sirloin

There is no basis to the contention that James I (as suggested by Jonathan Swift), or Henry VIII, Charles II, or any other English king 'knighted' a cut of beef, which thus became 'Sir Loin', although this myth is found in many popular books of etymology, and has given rise to a mistaken sequel, the *baron* (or double sirloin) of beef.

In reality the word, which was spelled *surloin* until 1600, dates from the 15th century and comes directly from Old French *surlonge*: *sur* – 'on' the *longe* – 'loin'; in Latin, *super lumbus*.

Tempura

Neither a native Japanese dish, nor, indeed, a Japanese name.

When the Portuguese arrived in the 17th century, the Japanese noticed that at certain 'times' (Portuguese, *tempora*) of the year, notably Lent,* they switched from meat to fish. With Oriental subtlety the Japanese concluded that the word for 'times' meant a variety of seafood.

* Siesta *also has a religious origin. The monastic day was punctuated by the canonical hours of prayer: matins, prime, nones, vespers, and so on. The 'sixth', or* sexta, *evolved into* siesta.

MAKING A NAME

UFUK RESTAURANT*
Izmir, Turkey
*Patronized by the Compiler.

Ufuk Restaurant, Izmir, Turkey

ULYSSES TYREBITER
Boston, Massachusetts

UNABLE TO FORNICATE*
Indian Chief
Northwestern U.S.

*Reported by Mencken. Fly-Fornication was a good
Puritan name, given to children born out of wedlock.

URBAN SHOCKER
Pitcher, New York Yankees
New York City

URE A. PIGG
Restaurateur
Portland, Oregon
(Oregon Journal)

URINE MCZEAL*
Washington County, Florida

*Compare Argo Pisson, Quality Control Engineer,
Raytheon Corporation, Lexington, Mass.; and Kitty Peed,
Cape Coral, Fla., who died in a light airplane accident.

URSULA WOOP
National Typewriting Champion
East Germany

U. S. BOND
Safe Deposit Manager
Harvard Trust Company
Cambridge, Massachusetts

VASELINE LOVE*
Jackson, Tennessee

Compare Love Kisses Love, mess attendant, U.S.S. Lexington, Vaseline Maleria, and Magnetic Love, secretary, U.S. Army Air Corps.

VENIAMIN DYMSHITS
Chairman, Gosplan
U.S.S.R.

MR. VENUS BONAPARTE
(The Times)

VERBAL FUNDERBURK*
Lakeland, Florida

Mrs. Funderburk wrote to a collaborator of the Compiler to ask if she had the funniest name in the world. Her anxieties were laid to rest.

PROFESSOR VERBAL SNOOK
Chairman, Mathematics Department
Oral Roberts University
Tulsa, Oklahoma

MR. VICE*
Malefactor
New Orleans, Louisiana

Arrested 820 times and convicted 421, probably a record (International Herald Tribune). The publisher of Law & Order, on the other hand, is Mr. Copp.

Mr. Vice, Malefactor, New Orleans

VILE ALBERT
St. Johnsbury, Vermont

VIOLET ORGAN *
Art Historian
New York City

*Biographer of the American painter Robert Henri. She
never married. Compare Violet Butt, Washington, D.C.

Vile Albert

VIRGINIA MAY SWEATT STRONG
Memphis, Tennessee

VOID NULL*
Schoolteacher
San Diego, California

Born 3 January 1904, in Mexico, Mo., to Henrietta and Thomas Jefferson Null, whose occupation is enigmatically given as 'panatorium'. Compare Romeo Zero, New York City.

Void Null

171

VOLUME DINGLE*
Tampa, Florida

His wife threw out his pants, containing his life's savings (Tampa Tribune). *Compare Elisha Peanut Tingle, Gumboro, Del.*

MR. VROOM*
Motorcycle Dealer
Port Elizabeth, South Africa

(New York Times)

Compare Joy Auto Collision, Toronto, and Fuzle-Rub Motor Training School, Calcutta.

WAMBLY BALD
Reporter, *New York Post*
New York City

WARREN PEACE
Williams College, Massachusetts

SIR W. C. DAMPIER-WHETHAM
Upwater Lodge, Cambridge

WELCOME BABY DARLING
Advertising Man
Greenwich, Connecticut

WILLIAM MCKINLEY LOUISIANA LEVEEBUST SMITH
Richmond, Virginia

Mr Vroom, Motorcycle Dealer, Port Elizabeth, South Africa

WUN TU O'CLOCK
Boston, Massachusetts

WYRE & TAPPING *
Detectives
New York City
The Compiler has a photograph of this establishment.

YELBERTON ABRAHAM TITTLE
Quarterback, New York Giants
New York City

ZEPPELIN W. WONG*
Attorney
San Francisco, California
*Fluent in Chinese and German.

ZEZOZOSE ZADFRACK*
California
*Natural son of C. Manson, Mass Murderer, by a
Miss Atkins.

ZILPHER SPITTLE
English parish record
(*Maclean's* magazine)

ZIP A-DEE-DOO DAUB*
La Luz, New Mexico

(The Miami Herald)

*Firstborn son of Mr. & Mrs. Daub, who waited 12 years to
have a baby, and stated that the name 'just seemed right'.*

ZODA VIOLA KLONTZ GAZOLA
U.S.A.

DR. ZOLTAN OVARY*
Gynaecologist, New York Hospital
New York City
And, of course, Madame Ovary.

ZOWIE BOWIE *

(Times Literary Supplement)

* *Son of rock singer David Bowie.*

IMBROGLIOS

Tumbling the Plumber

BELGRADE – A Belgrade plumber, Mr. Miodrag Jocic, who was called to attend to the sink in the home of a newly married couple, ended up in hospital with concussion and a broken leg.

The wife was out when Mr. Jocic arrived at the house. When she returned, she found a pair of legs sticking out from under the sink, and thought they belonged to her husband. Exactly what she did next is not certain, but it caused the plumber to bang his head into the sink above him.

The ambulance arrived to take him to hospital and while he was being carried down the stairs on a stretcher, one of the ambulance men asked him what had happened. On being told, he was so convulsed with laughter that he dropped the stretcher and the plumber tumbled down the stairs and broke a leg.

He is in hospital now, threatening to sue. The husband says that the incident so upset his wife that she will have nothing to do with him. – *The Times*

Plat du Jour

ZURICH – Hans and Erna W., who asked the mass circulation *Blick* newspaper not to print their full name took their poodle Rosa along with them to an evening meal in Hong Kong.

They asked a waiter over to the table. After

Plat du jour

ordering, they pointed to the poodle while they made eating motions to show they wanted it to be fed.

Eventually the waiter took Rosa off into the kitchen. Later he came back with their main dish and when they picked up the silver lid they found their poodle roasted inside, garnished with pepper sauce and bamboo shoots.

The couple returned to Zurich immediately. – *Reuter*

Fire Drill

PHILADELPHIA – The Lacey Park and Southampton volunteer fire departments set an abandoned row-house complex ablaze in Warminster Heights, Bucks County, Monday night so that they could practice putting it out.

By the time they did put the fire out, 150 residents of nearby buildings had had to be evacuated, the electricity of all Warminster Heights had been out for several hours, firemen had been called in from five neighbouring communities and the Johnsville Naval Air Base, and there had been extensive smoke, heat, and water damage to nearby buildings and cars.

What the Lacey Park and Southampton firemen had discovered, just after setting the fire, was that they did not have any water.

'Boy, that was really dumb,' said a Dean Street resident, Mrs. Roy Hopkins, who watched the blaze with her daughter.

'Yeah, it was dumb,' agreed Mrs. Karen Zeno of the nearby Ashwood Apartments.* – Philadelphia *Inquirer*

---

* *Firefighters in the West were also beset, as reported in the* Washington Post *in February 1977.*

'For the last seven months, the National Park Service has been trying to put out a fire in a 25,000-year accumulation of giant sloth dung in a remote Grand Canyon cave.'

'So far the agency has not succeeded, and the effort has cost $50,000.

. . . Smithsonian Institution paleobiology curator Dr. Clayton Ray said . . . the Shasta sloth – which he does not like to call a giant sloth "because

178

he was only about the size of a black bear, nothing huge" – was not very notable except for producing a large and durable stool in the same place for about 25,000 years.'

Harassment

A conservatively dressed man who boarded the Seventh Avenue Subway at the Times Square station was the victim of a strange assault, reported by *The New York Times* in March 1969.

He was followed by a weird youth with frizzy hair who suddenly stuck his foot in the door, preventing the train from departing. Pointing his finger at the gentleman, he screamed over and over, 'Give me back my yo-yo!'

The gentleman maintained a dignified silence.

Finally another passenger, announcing that he had to get to work, pushed the deranged youth's foot away, the doors closed, the train pulled out of the station.

Just below Thirty-fourth Street the gentleman reached into his coat pocket and, smiling enigmatically, began to spin a large, red yo-yo.

The Last Words of General Sedgwick

'Come, come!' said the general stoutly to some men who were dodging about under the enemy's fire.*

'Why, they couldn't hit an elephant at this dist . . . '

* *At Spotsylvania, May 9, 1864.*
Cf. O. W. Holmes, Touched With Fire. *Cambridge: Harvard University Press,.1947.*

MEDICINE

Delirium

'Out of the furrow' (*lira*) in Latin – referring to a reeling plowman. 'Off his trolley', we would say.

Grog

Grog is named after the unpopular Vice-Admiral Edward Vernon of the Royal Navy, who fought in the War of Jenkins' Ear. He was a friend of George Washington's brother, whence Mount Vernon.

The Royal Navy customarily doled out a daily tot of rum to the tars, but in 1740 the admiral ordered that water be added to make it harder for them to get drunk. This made him more unpopular than ever.

He was known as 'Old Grog' because of his *grogram* cloak (from the French *gros grain*, 'rough cloth'), and his nickname stuck to the drink.

Quack

As the bubonic plague, for which there was no cure, decimated Europe, swarms of bogus healers preyed on the desperate populace. Some offered ointments or salves (from Latin *salve*, 'save'). Their noisy sales talks, like those of carnival barkers, reminded the Dutch of ducks quacking (*kwakken*). So in Holland they became known as *quacksalvers*, and later *quacks*.

Their Italian confreres, like our soap-box orators, made a practice of mounting the nearest bench (whence *mountebank*, a 'charlatan') to extol their own brand of salve or *nostrum* (Latin for 'our'). In Italy an epidemic was thought to result from the 'influence' (*influenza*, our *flu*) of a malign conjuncture of planets.

℞

In Roman times prescriptions often began with a prayer to Jupiter. Since then they have continued to be written in Latin, but the prayer has shrunk to Jupiter's astrological sign, ℞. Another theory is that ℞ is an abbreviation for the Latin *recipe*, 'take'.

Venom

The Indo-European *ven* or *wen*, 'want' or 'desire', led to Latin *venari*, 'to hunt', which in turn gave rise to *venison*.

It also brought forth *Venus*, the 'venerated' or beloved.

Venice, in turn, took its name from a tribe who called themselves *Veneti*: the 'desirables', so to speak, just as the current inhabitants enjoy being called the 'beautiful people'. From *Venice* came *Venezuela*, 'little Venice'.

A goblet of *Venice* glass was supposed to break when filled with *venom*,* which originally meant a potion to facilitate lovemaking or *venery*; whence *venereal*, having to do with lovemaking.

* *I like Frederick ('Baron Corvo') Rolfe's description of a poisoned glove as a 'gauntlet envenomed'.*

181

APPENDICES

Terms of Multitude

Every occupation – law, medicine, the sea, agriculture, electronics – has its own precise terminology. Without it, business could not be conducted. That each uses its own set of plurals is, therefore, no surprise. Several vessels for the sailor make a *fleet*, not a *herd*; we have a *library* of books; a *congregation* of worshippers (from Latin *grex*, 'flock'); a *portfolio* of securities; and so on.

These words, usually called collective or generic terms or nouns of multitude, are only surprising to an outsider. The English have always liked to make lists of them, starting with the courtesy (i.e., etiquette) books of the late Middle Ages.* Here are the most important ones traditionally used of animals, notably in hunting and hawking. The terms are frequently interchanged.

*And invent new ones, e.g., a *flourish* of strumpets, a *chapter* of trollops, an *anthology* of pros, a *smelting* of 'ores.

A *colony* of ants
A *shrewdness* or *troop* of apes
A *pace* of asses
A *cete* of badgers
A *shoal* of bass
A *sloth* of bears
A *colony* of beaver †
A *swarm* of bees
A *dissimulation* of birds
A *singular* of boars (cf. page 187)
A *clouder* of cats (often corrupted into *clowder*; perhaps originally *cluster*)
An *army* of caterpillars
A *drove* of cattle
A *brood* of chickens (but a *clutch* of eggs)
A *rag* of colts

A *cover* of coot
A *murder* of crows
A *cowardice* of curs
A *dole* (formerly *dule*) or *piteousness* of doves or turtledoves
A *paddling* of duck (swimming)
A *raft* of duck (collected in the water, e.g., to sleep)
A *team* of duck (in flight)
A *herd* of elephants
A *gang* of elk
A *business* of ferrets or flies *
A *charm* of finches
A *school* of fish **
A *skulk* or *troop* (and sometimes *cloud* or *earth*) of foxes (which, however, are solitary animals)

A herd of elephants

A *gaggle* of geese (stationary)
A *skein* of geese (flying)
A *trip* of goats
A *cluster* of grasshoppers
A *husk* of hare
A *cast* of hawks (two)
A *brood* of hens
A *siege* of herons

A *drift* of hogs
A *harras* of (stud) horses (still
    used in Latin languages)
A *pack* of hounds
A *party* of jays
A *swarm* of insects
A *troop* of kangaroos
A *kindle* or *litter* of kittens

A *deceit* of lapwings
An *exaltation*, *ascension*, or *bevy*
   of larks
A *leap* of leopards
A *pride* of lions
A *plague* or *swarm* of locusts
A *tidings* of magpies
A *sord* of mallards
A *stud* (sic) of mares
A *richness* of martens
A *nest* of mice
A *troop* or *shrewdness* of monkeys
A *barren* of mules (perhaps
   originally *bearing* or *burden)*
A *watch* of nightingales
A *parliament* of owls
A *litter* of partridge
A *covey* of quail
A *muster* or *ostentation* of
   peacocks
A *nye* or *covey* of pheasants (on
   the ground)
A *bouquet* of pheasants (rising)
A *congregation* of plovers
A *string* of ponies

A *litter* of pups
A *nest* of rabbits
An *unkindness* of ravens
A *crash* of rhinoceroses
A *bevy* of roebucks
A *building* of rooks
A *pod* of seal (or *harem* of
   females)
A *flock* of sheep
A *bed* of snakes
A *wisp* or *walk* of snipe
A *host* of sparrows
A *dray* of squirrels
A *murmuration* of sandpipers or
   starlings
A *sounder* of swine
A *spring* of teal
A *knot* of toads
A *rafter* of turkeys
A *bale* of turtles
A *nest* of vipers or wasps
A *pod* or *gam* of whales
A *pack* or *route* of wolves
A *fall* of woodcock
A *descent* of woodpeckers

† *The final s is often omitted when an animal is thought of as game.*
* *A* freamyng *of ferrets occurs in Sladen's* The Complete Crossword Reference
Book, London, 1949, *in a list of collective nouns, along with* pride *of lions and
so on. It is found nowhere else. Nuttall's* Standard Dictionary, *Fifth Edition,
London, 1932–50, has* fesning, *from which Sladen copied it incorrectly. Nuttall,
in turn, miscopied it from* fesymes *in Beard's* American Boys' Book of Wild
Animals, *Philadelphia, 1921. This is apparently an error for* fesynes, *which
occurs in Strutt's* The Sports and Pastimes of the People of England, *London,
1838. That, in turn, is a misprint for* besynes *(i.e.* business*) of ferrets, which
occurs in the 15th century* Book of Saint Albans.
** Originally *shoal.*

Rhyming Slang

We often don't realize how many expressions are Cockney rhyming
slang. The principle is illustrated by calling a girl a 'twist and twirl'

(usually shortened to 'twist'), or a wife, 'trouble and strife', and so on. Thus 'facts' in Cockney became *brass tacks*, as in our 'let's get down to brass tacks'.

'Beer' became *pig's ear*.

La-de-dah refers to someone fancy enough to own a 'car'.

'Eat' became *Dutch treat*, from 'Dutch Street', where there were a number of eating places.

'No hope' became *no soap*.

'Fart' became *raspberry tart*, as in 'Give 'em the *raspberry*,' or *razz*.

'Go' became *scapa flow* or *scapa*. This expression overlaps *scarper* (Parlyaree – circus language – meaning to desert a play or quit one's lodgings without paying). *Scarper* comes from the Italian *scappare* 'escape', from the Latin *excappa*, to slip 'out of one's cape' when arrested. *Scarper* has another sense, soft footwear (in which to escape the police), presumably influenced by Italian *scarpa*, 'shoe'.

Grand Tour Words

Words sometimes set forth from one country and after sojourns abroad reappear quite changed. I have never seen a list of such 'round trip' expressions, so they are hard to collect; one just has to be alert as one goes along.

French *boeuf*, 'beef', for example, sallied forth to England with the Normans, was accepted as *beefsteak*, and recently returned to the Académie Française dictionary as *biftek*.

Some women may be aware that what we call a *redingote* is the French word for our *riding coat*, having come back around a circular course. Few citizens of Genoa, however, know that their blue *jeans* are named after the English pronunciation of the French name, *Gênes*, for their own city. Nor are the burghers of Nîmes conscious that the *denim* their jeans are made from came centuries ago from Nîmes itself (*de Nîmes*). Still another fabric, *mohair*, or goat's wool cloth, emigrated to France as *moiré*, and was reintegrated into English as *moire*, or watered silk.

Many words have been altered by a sojourn south of the border. For example, a Frenchman speaking of *mariachi* music is referring to *les mariages*, at which it was played when the French occupied Mexico. A *freebooter* is a highwayman or land pirate. In Central America he became known as a *filibustero*. The word returned to America as *filibuster*, and acquired its new sense of a drawn-out oration.

Travellers to India who stay in a *bungalow* are often unaware that the English word started out there as *Bangalore*.

Un coctel, from our 'cocktail', is now good French; it may derive from American Creole *cocktay*, from French *coquetier*, the 'egg-cup' in which it was served; alternatively, it may be a word from West Africa, where it has also returned.

For *grog*, see page 180.

The young man who today accompanies a Frenchman playing golf, was in his earlier days a *cadet*, 'youth', who made his way to Scotland, was rechristened a *caddie*, and then returned to the golf courses of France as *le caddie*.

For *flirt*, see page 35.

Many Grand Tour words are the labels put by Portuguese explorers to what they found in their travels, which later returned to Europe as authentic native imports.

Caste is Portuguese *casta*, 'chaste' or 'pure'.

Cobra is from the Portuguese word for 'snake'.

Fetish is Portuguese *feitiço*, from the Latin *facticius*, a 'made thing'.

A *joss* stick is Portuguese *deos*, from the Latin *deus*,* 'god'.

Corral is Portuguese *curral*, from the Dutch *kraal*.

Mandarin is Portuguese *mandarim*, from a Malay word meaning an 'official'.

Palaver is Portuguese *palavra*, 'word'.

Tank is Portuguese *tanque*, a 'pool' or 'cistern'.

For *tempura*, see page 165.

* Dyaus, *the Sanskrit word for 'day' and 'heaven', is in turn the source of* Zeus, deus, Jupiter *(day-father), and* Tiu, *son of Odin in Nordic myth, and the god of war.* Tiu, *in turn gave us* Tuesday, *which corresponds to French* mardi, *'Tuesday', from Latin* Mars, *also the god of war.*

Redundancies

Throughout history many redundancies, or pleonasms, arose when new arrivals questioned local inhabitants about names for things.

Thus, Torpenow Hill, near Plymouth, England, means 'hill hill hill hill': Saxon *tor*, Celtic *pen*, Scandinavian *how* and Middle English *hill*.

Act I
Saxon invader: What do you call that *tor*?

Celt: A *pen*, of course.
Saxon invader: Right, we'll call it Tor Pen.

Act II
Viking invader: You! What's that *how* called?
Saxon descendant: Torpen.
Viking: Okay, from now on it's Torpen How.

Act III
Middle Englishman: I say, what do you call that hill over there?
Viking descendant: Well, sir, we folks hereabouts call it Torpenow, we
          does.
Middle Englishman: Indeed! Well, as you like. Torpenow Hill it is.

Mt. Pendleton, Maine, contains three words for 'hill'.

Similarly, when Captain Cook asked the name of an Australian marsupial, the natives answered *kangaroo*, meaning 'I don't know'. And the French word for 'transom' is *vasistas* – German for 'What's that?'

For *Admiral of the Ocean Sea* cf. note, page 51.

The river *Avon* means river 'River'.

A *cheerful countenance* means a 'faceful face'. *Cheer*, Middle English 'face', comes from the French *chère*, 'face', as in *faire bonne chère*, 'be of good cheer'.

A *demitasse cup* is a 'half cup cup'.

Dishevelled hair means 'unhaired hair'.

Dry Sack means 'dry dry'. *Sack* comes from French *sec*, 'dry'; whence German *Sekt*, champagne.

Marline line is 'tying line line'.

A *mess mate* is a 'food food': French *mets*, 'food', plus a variation of 'meat'.

A *pea jacket* is a 'jacket jacket', from the Dutch *pij*, a sailor's garment.

Prosciutto ham is 'ham ham'.

Reindeer comes from Old Norse *hreinn*, 'reindeer', and *dyr*, 'deer'.

The Sahara Desert is 'desert desert'.

A *saltcellar* comes from the French *salière*, salt dispenser, and so means 'salt salter'.

Shrimps scampi are 'shrimps shrimps'.

A *singular of boars* (cf. Terms of Multitude) comes from the French *sanglier*, 'boar', and is thus a 'boar of boars'.

Niger is Berber for 'river', so the River Niger is the 'river river'.

Reduplications

Fiddle-faddle: Fiddle is a corruption of *Vitula*, the Roman goddess of victory and jubilation, which are often accompanied by music.

Hobson-jobson: On the holy day of Ashura the faithful cry out, '*Ya Hasan, Ya Husein*', to mourn the murder of the two grandsons of Mohammed. British army slang turned this into *hobson-jobson*, which sounded more reasonable, meaning a hubbub or tumult. Any folk-etymology is thus called a *hobson-jobson*.

Hocus-pocus: From *hic est corpus*, 'this is the body' in the Roman mass. *Hoax* is a contraction of *hocus*. (*Patter* meaning a 'rapid-fire spiel', comes from the Latin name for the Lord's Prayer, *Pater noster*, 'Our Father'.)

Hugger-mugger: This term for mysterious skulduggery is a variation of *hoker-moker*, from Middle English *mokeren*, 'conceal'.

Hurly-burly: This 16th-century expression for 'uproar' evolved from *hurling* (fighting) *and hurling*, a 15th-century jingle. There is presumably a connection with *hurluberlu*, which occurs in Rabelais, and Greek *hurliburli*, 'headlong'. One thinks with satisfaction of Mrs. Pat Campbell's description of marriage as a transfer from 'the hurly-burly of the chaise longue to the decorum of the double bed'.

Mumbo jumbo: Originally a tribal god, priest, or fetish of the Mandingos of the western Sudan. The name apparently derives from *Mama*, a 'grandmother' or 'ancestor', and *dyambo*, 'headdress' (or perhaps *gyo*, 'trouble', and *mbo*, 'leave').

Nitty-gritty: Originally, black slang for the inner end of the vagina.

Surprising Family Names

Adam(s): Hebrew, 'red'.*

* *There were plenty of red-haired or red-skinned people in Britain at the time surnames were assigned, but the colour is almost always camouflaged, as Reid, Rudd, Rowse, Rous, Rouse, Rose, Russell, Rufus, Gough, or some other variant.*

Algernon: Moustached. A particular given name of the Percy family, applied at a time when moustaches were unusual.

Atterbury: At the fort. *Ter* is the obsolete feminine dative singular of 'the'.

Bedford: Probably battle-ford.

Blood: From Welsh *Ap-Lud*, 'Son of Lud' or 'Ludwig'.

Brock: Badger.

Calvert: Calfherd.

Cameron: Gaelic, 'hook-nose'.

Cass: Diminutive of *Cassandra*, a feminine form of *Alexander*.

Cecil: From Latin *caecus*, 'blind'. *Sheila* is from the same source via *Cecilia*.

Cheever: Old French, 'she-goat'.

Coffin: French *chauvin*, 'bald'.

Coward: Cowherd.

Denis(e): Follower of Dionysius.

Devereux: French 'from Evreux', which took its name from the Celtic tribe known as the Eburuci because they lived on the River Ebura (or Eure), which, in turn, comes from the word for 'yew tree' in Gaulish.

Fitch: Polecat.

Hollister: A female brothel-keeper* or madam (in the masculine, *Hollyer*).

**Many English occupation names add an 's' to give the feminine form: e.g. Baker-Baxter; Spinner-Spinster; Webber-Webster.*

Kellogg: Kill-hog; a hog butcher.

Kennedy: 'Hideous head' in Irish.

Lazar: 'Leper', Lazarus.

MacArthur: Son of Arthur; but see page 70.

Morpeth: 'Murder-path', where someone was killed.

Pendleton: From Pen Hill, i.e., 'hill hill', see page 186.

Popper: On an envelope, *Frankfort* can be abbreviated *FF*; in Hebrew, which has no separate capital *F*, this is written *PP*. Over time, persons who lived in *PP* were eventually called *Popper*.

Powell: Welsh *Ap-Howell*, 'son of Howell', just as *Pugh* comes from *AP-Hugh*.

Purcell: French *purcel*, 'little pig'.

Satterlee, Salterleigh: From *saetere*, 'robber'.

Seward: Sowherd.

Walker: Not, as one might suppose, the guardian of a village (who was the *ward*); rather, the man who trampled the cloth being bleached in the vat of the *fuller*.

INDEX

Garden 135
von Garlic 57
garnish 104
Garrison 109
Gash 137
Gazola 174
Gemorah 154
generic terms 182
genteelisms xx, 118
Gesundheit 79
Ghostly 108
Glasscock 57, 136
Glomp 156
Gluck 59
God 21, 125
Goedebed 96'
Goldfarb 156
Goo 139
Good 98
Goon 40
gossamer 145
grand tour words 185
Green, Joseph Henry 87
Greenblatt 151
Greene 43
grog 180
Grubb 79
Gryp 44
Guppy 122

Habakkuk 63
Hamburger 111
Hankey 94
Harbor 135
Hardy, Godfrey Harold 142
Hare 59
Harison 57
Harris 80, 139
hazard(s) 134
Headline 58
Hee 156
Heine 25, 140
Hell 124
Hildebiddle 96
hip, hip, hurray 91
Hogg 77
Hollister 189
Hontas 96
hooker 52
Hooker 42, 80

Hooton 122
Horsey 62
humble pie 162
Humboldt, Alexander von 143
Hunnybun 43
Hymen 65

Ibsen, Hebric 86
Integration 139

Jackson 2, 109
Jefferson, Thomas 29
Jejeebhoy 79
Jocic, Miodrag 176
Jockitch 79
John XXIII, Pope 115
Johnson 137
Jones 24, 43, 156
Joynt 81
Jullien 97

Kaplan 73
Karamanov 79
Katz Pajama Co 81
Kawakami, Otoichi 49
Keel 41
Kellogg 189
Kennedy 190
ketchup 162
King 123
Klinkenberg 4
Kluemper 96
Krapp 81
Kunt 112

Lane 109
Lawless & Lynch 2, 95
Lawrence 108
Lazar 190
Leake 110
Lear 150
Lemon 125
Ley 45
Lobo 96
loo 118
lord 52
Love 10, 125, 139, 168
lumber 119
luncheon 162
Lurch 55